Letters of Abelard and Heloise

To which is prefix'd

A PARTICULAR ACCOUNT

OF THEIR

Lives, Amours, and Misfortunes.

BY THE LATE JOHN HUGHES, ESQ.

Together with the

POEM OF ELOISA TO ABELARD.

BY MR. POPE.

And, (to which is now added) the

POEM OF ABELARD TO ELOISA,

BY MRS. MADAN.

D0104665

Contents

Preface

It is very surprising that the *Letters of Abelard and Heloise* have not sooner appeared in English, since it is generally allowed, by all who have seen them in other languages, that they are written with the greatest passion of any in this kind which are extant. And it is certain that the *Letters from a Nun to a Cavalier*, which have so long been known and admired among us, are in all respects inferior to them. Whatever those were, these are known to be genuine Pieces occasioned by an amour which had very extraordinary consequences, and made a great noise at the time when it happened, being between two of the most distinguished Persons of that age.

These *Letters*, therefore, being truly written by the Persons themselves, whose names they bear, and who were both remarkable for their genius and learning, as well as by a most extravagant passion for each other, are every where full of sentiments of the heart, (which are not to be imitated in a feigned story,) and touches of Nature, much more moving than any which could flow from the Pen of a Writer of Novels, or enter into the imagination of any who had not felt the like emotions and distresses.

They were originally written in Latin, and are extant in a Collection of the Works of *Abelard*, printed at Paris in the year 1616. With what elegance and beauty of stile they were written in that language, will sufficiently appear to the learned Reader, even by those few citations which are set at the bottom of the page in some places of the following history. But the Book here mentioned consisting chiefly of school-divinity, and the learning of those times, and therefore being rarely to be met with but in public libraries, and in the hands of some learned men, the Letters of *Abelard* and *Heloise* are much more known by a Translation, or rather Paraphrase of them, in French, first published at the Hague in 1693, and which afterwards received several other more complete Editions. This Translation is much applauded, but who was the Author of it is not certainly known. Monsieur Bayle says he had been informed it was done by a woman; and, perhaps, he thought no one besides could have entered so thoroughly into the passion and tenderness of such writings, for which that sex seems to have a more natural disposition than the other. This may be judged of by the Letters themselves, among which those of *Heloise* are the most moving, and the Master seems in this particular to have been excelled by the Scholar.

In some of the later Editions in French, there has been prefixed to the Letters an Historical Account of *Abelard* and *Heloise*; this is chiefly extracted from the Preface of the Editor of *Abelard's* Works in Latin, and from the *Critical Dictionary* of Monsieur Bayle,[1] who has put together, under several articles, all the particulars he was able to collect concerning these two famous Persons; and though the first Letter of *Abelard to Philintus*, in which he relates his own story, may seem to have rendered this account in part unnecessary; yet the Reader will not be displeased to see the thread of the relation entire, and continued to the death of the Persons whose misfortunes had made their lives so very remarkable.

It is indeed impossible to be unmoved at the surprising and multiplied afflictions and persecutions which befel a man of *Abelard's* fine genius, when we see them so feelingly described by his own hand. Many of these were owing to the malice of such as were his enemies on the account of his superior learning and merit; yet the great calamities of his life took their rise from his unhappy indulgence of a criminal passion, and giving himself a loose to unwarrantable pleasures. After this he was perpetually involved in sorrow and distress, and in vain sought for ease and quiet in a monastic life. The *Letters* between him and his beloved *Heloise* were not written till long after their marriage and separation, and when each of them was dedicated to a life of religion. Accordingly we find in them surprising mixtures of devotion and tenderness, and remaining frailty, and a lively picture of human nature in its contrarieties of passion and reason, its infirmities, and its sufferings.

---

[1] *Vide Artic.* Abelard, Heloise, Foulques, *and* Paraclete

The History of Abelard and Heloise

Peter Abelard was born in the village of Palais in Britany. He lived in the twelfth century, in the reigns of *Louis the Gross*, and *Louis the Young*. His Father's name was *Beranger*, a gentleman of a considerable and wealthy family. He took care to give his children a liberal and pious education, especially his eldest son *Peter*, on whom he endeavoured to bestow all possible improvements, because there appeared in him an extraordinary vivacity of wit joined with sweetness of temper, and all imaginable presages of a great man.

When he had made some advancement in learning, he grew so fond of his books, that, lest affairs of the world might interrupt his proficiency in them, he quitted his birthright to his younger brothers, and applied himself entirely to the studies of Philosophy and Divinity.

Of all the sciences to which he applied himself, that which pleased him most, and in which he made the greatest progress, was Logick. He had a very subtile wit, and was incessantly whetting it by disputes, out of a restless ambition to be master of his weapons. So that in a short time he gained the reputation of the greatest philosopher of his age; and has always been esteemed the founder of what we call the *Learning of the Schoolmen*.

He finished his studies at Paris, where learning was then in a flourishing condition. In this city he found that famous professor of philosophy William des Champeaux, and soon became his favourite scholar; but this did not last long. The professor was so hard put to it to answer the subtle objections of his new scholar, that he grew uneasy with him. The school soon run into parties. The senior scholars, transported with envy against *Abelard*, seconded their master's resentment. All this served only to increase the young man's presumption, who now thought himself sufficiently qualified to set up a school of his own. For this purpose he chose an advantageous place, which was the town of Melun, ten leagues from Paris, where the French court resided at that time. Champeaux did all that he could to hinder the erecting of this school; but some of the great courtiers being his enemies, the opposition he made to it only promoted the design of his rival.

~ 3 ~

Pierre Abelard

The reputation of this new professor made a marvellous progress, and eclipsed that of Champeaux. These successes swelled *Abelard* so much that he removed his school to Corbeil, in order to engage his enemy the more closer in more frequent disputations. But his excessive application to study brought upon him a long and dangerous sickness, which constrained him to return to his own native air.

After he had spent two years in his own country he made a second adventure to Paris, where he found that his old antagonist Champeaux had resigned his chair to another, and was retired into a convent of Canons Regular, among whom he continued his lectures. *Abelard* attacked him with such fury, that he quickly forced him to renounce his tenets. Whereupon the poor monk became so despicable, and his antagonist in such great esteem, that nobody went to the lectures of Champeaux, and the very man who succeeded him in his professorship, listed under *Abelard*, and became his scholar.

He was scarce fixed in his chair before he found himself exposed more than ever to the strokes of the most cruel envy. Endeavours were used to do him ill offices by all those who were any ways disaffected to him. Another professor was put into his place, who had thought it his duty to submit to *Abelard*, in short so many enemies were raised against him that he was forced to retreat from Paris to Melun, and there revived his logick lectures. But this held not long; for hearing that Champeaux with all his infantry was retired into a country village, he came and posted himself on mount St. Genevieve, where he erected a new school, like a kind of battery against him whom Champeaux had left to teach at Paris.

Champeaux understanding that his substitute was thus besieged in his school, brought the Regular Canons attack again to their monastery. But this, instead of relieving his friend, caused all his scholars to desert him. At which the poor philosopher was so mortified, that he followed the example of his patron Champeaux, and turned monk too.

The dispute now lay wholly between Abelard and Champeaux, who renewed it with great warmth on both sides; but the senior had not the best on't. While it was depending, *Abelard* was obliged to visit his father and mother, who, according to the fashion of those times, had resolved to forsake the world, and retire into convents, in order to devote themselves more seriously to the care of their salvation.

Having assisted at the admission of his parents into their respective monasteries and received their blessing, he returned to Paris, where during his absence, his rival had been promoted to the bishoprick of Chalons. And now being in a condition to quit his school without any suspicions of flying from his enemy, he resolved to apply himself wholly to Divinity.

To this end he removed to Laon, where one *Anselm* read divinity-lectures with good reputation. But *Abelard* was so little satisfied with the old man's abilities, who has he says, had a very mean genius, and a great fluency of words without sense, that he took a resolution for the future to hear no other master than the Holy Scriptures. A good resolution! if a man takes the Spirit of God for his guide, and be more concerned to distinguish truth from falsehood, than to confirm himself in those principles into which his, own fancy or complexion, or the prejudices of his birth and education, have insensibly led him.

Abelard, together with the Holy Scriptures, read the ancient fathers and doctors of the church, in which he spent whole days and nights, and profited so well, that instead of returning to *Anselm's* lectures, he took up the same employment, and began to explain the Prophet *Ezekiel* to some of his fellow-pupils. He performed this part so agreeably; and in so easy a method that he soon got a crowd of auditors.

The jealous *Anselm* could not bear this; he quickly found means to get the lecturer silenced. Upon this *Abelard* removed to Paris once more, where he proceeded with his public exposition on Ezekiel, and soon acquired the same reputation for his divinity he had before gained for his philosophy. His eloquence and learning procured him an incredible number of scholars from all parts; so that if he had minded saving of money, he might have grown rich with ease in a short time. And happy had it been for him, if, among all the enemies his learning exposed him to, he had guarded his heart against the charms of love. But, alas! the greatest doctors are not always the wisest men, as appears from examples in every age; but from none more remarkable than that of this learned man, whose story I am now going to tell you.

Pierre Abelard

Abelard, besides his uncommon merit as a scholar, had all the accomplishments of a gentleman. He had a greatness of soul which nothing could shock; his passions were delicate, his judgment solid, and his taste exquisite. He was of a graceful person, and carried himself with the air of a man of quality. His conversation was sweet, complaisant, easy, and gentleman-like. It seemed as tho' Nature had designed him for a more elevated employment than that of teaching the sciences. He looked upon riches and grandeur with contempt, and had no higher ambition than to make his name famous among learned men, and to be reputed the greatest doctor of his age: but he had human frailty, and all his philosophy could not guard him from the attacks of love. For some time indeed, he had defended himself against this passion pretty well, when the temptation was but slight; but upon a more intimate familiarity with such agreeable objects, he found his reason fail him: yet in respect to his wisdom, he thought of compounding the matter and resolved at first, that love and philosophy should dwell together in the same breast. He intended only to let out his heart to the former, and that but for a little while; never considering that love is a great ruiner of projects; and that when it has once got a share in a heart, it is easy to possess itself of the whole.

He was now in the seven or eight and twentieth year of his age, when he thought himself completely happy in all respects, excepting that he wanted a mistress. He considered therefore of making a choice, but such a one as might be most suitable to his notions, and the design he had of passing agreeably those hours he did not employ in his study. He had several ladies in his eye, to whom as he says in one of his *Letters*, he could easily have recommended himself. For you must understand, that besides his qualifications mentioned before, he had a vein of poetry, and made abundance of little easy songs, which he would sing with all the advantage of a gallant air and pleasant voice. But tho' he was cut out for a lover, he was not over-hasty in determining his choice. He was not of a humour to be pleased with the wanton or forward; he scorned easy pleasures, and sought to encounter with difficulties and impediments, that he might conquer with the greater glory. In short, he had not yet seen the woman he was to love.

Not far from the place where *Abelard* read his lectures lived one *Doctor Fulbert*, a canon of the church of Notre-Dame. This canon had

~ 6 ~

a niece named *Heloise* in his house whom he educated with great care and affection. Some writers say,[2] that she was the good man's natural daughter; but that, to prevent a public scandal, he gave out that she was his niece by his sister, who upon her death-bed had charged him with her education. But though it was well known in those times, as well as since, that the niece of an ecclesiastick is sometimes more nearly related to him, yet of this damsel's birth and parentage we have nothing very certain. There is reason to think, from one of her *Letters to Abelard*, that she came of a mean family; for she owns that great honour was done to her side by this alliance, and that he married much below himself. So that what Francis d'Amboise says, that she was of the name and family of Montmorency has no manner of foundation. It is very probable she was really and truly Fulbert's niece, as he affirmed her to be. Whatever she was for birth, she was a very engaging woman; and if she was not a perfect beauty, she appeared such at least in *Abelard's* eyes. Her person was well proportioned, her features regular, her eyes sparkling, her lips vermillion and well formed, her complexion animated, her air fine, and her aspect sweet and agreeable. She had a surprising quickness of wit, an incredible memory, and a considerable share of learning, joined with humility; and all these accomplishments were attended with something so graceful and moving, that it was impossible for those who kept her company not to be in love with her.

As soon as *Abelard* had seen her, and conversed with her, the charms of her wit and beauty made such an impression upon his heart, that he presently conceived a most violent passion for her, and resolved to make it his whole endeavour to win her affections. And now, he that formerly quitted his patrimony to pursue his studies, laid aside all other engagements to attend his new passion.

In vain did Philosophy and Reason importune him to return; he was deaf to their call, and thought of nothing but how to enjoy the sight and company of his dear *Heloise*. And he soon met with the luckiest opportunity in the world. Fulbert who had the greatest affection imaginable for his niece, finding her to have a good share of natural wit, and a particular genius for learning, thought himself obliged to improve the talents which Nature had so liberally bestowed on her. He had already put her to learn several languages, which she

---

[2] Papyr. Maffo. Annal. 1. 3. *Joannes Canonicus Pariflus, Heloysiam naturalem filiam habebat prastanti ingenio formaque.*

quickly came to understand so well, that her fame began to spread itself abroad, and the wit and learning of *Heloise* was every where discoursed of. And though her uncle for his own share was no great scholar, he was very felicitous that his niece should have all possible improvements. He was willing, therefore, she should have masters to instruct her in what she had a mind to learn: but he loved his money, and this kept him from providing for her education so well as she desired.

Abelard, who knew *Heloise's* inclinations, and the temper of her uncle, thought this an opportunity favourable to his design. He was already well acquainted with Fulbert, as being his brother canon in the same church; and he observed how fond the other was of his friendship, and what an honour he esteemed it to be intimate with a person of his reputation. He therefore told him one day in familiarity, that he was at a loss for some house to board in; and if you could find room for me, said he, in yours, I leave to you name the terms.

The good man immediately considering that by this means he should provide an able master for his niece who, instead of taking money of him, offered to provide him well for his board, embraced his proposal with the joy imaginable, gave him a thousand caresses, and desired he would consider him for the future as one ambitious of the strictest friendship with him.

What an unspeakable joy was this to the amorous *Abelard*! to consider that he was going to live with her, who was the only object of his desires! that he should have the opportunity of seeing and conversing with her every day, and of acquainting her with his passion! However, he concealed his joy at present lest he should make his intention suspected. We told you before how liberal Nature had been to our lover in making his person every way so agreeable; so that he flattered himself that it was almost impossible[3] that any woman should reject his addresses. Perhaps he was mistaken: the sex has variety of humour. However, consider him as a philosopher who had therto lived in a strict chastity,[4] he certainly reasoned well in the business of love; when he concluded that *Heloise* would be an easier conquest to him than others because her learning gave him an

---

[3] *Tanti quippe tune nominis eram & juventutis & forma gratia praeminebam, ut quamcunque foeminartn nostre dignarer amore nullam verer repulsam.* 1 Epist. Abel. p. 10. Abel.
[4] *Froena libidini coepi laxare, qui antea viveram continantissime.* Ibid.

opportunity of establishing a correspondence by letters, in which he might discover his passion with greater freedom than he dared presume to use in conversation.

Some time after the Canon had taken *Abelard* into his own house, as they were discoursing one day about things somewhat above Fulbert's capacity, the latter turned the discourse insensibly to the good qualities of his niece; he informed *Abelard* of the excellency of her wit, and how strong a propensity she had to improve in learning; and withal made it his earnest request, that he would take the pains to instruct her. *Abelard* pretended to be surprised at a proposal of this nature. He told him that learning was not the proper business of women; that such inclinations in them had more of humour or curiosity than a solid desire of knowledge; and could hardly pass, among either the learned or ignorant, without drawing upon them the imputation of conceit and affectation. Fulbert answered, that this was very true of women of common capacities; but he hoped, when he had discoursed with his niece, and found what progress she had made already, and what a capacity she had for learning, he would be of another opinion. *Abelard* assured him, he was ready to do all he could for her improvement, and if she was not like other women, who hate to learn any thing beyond their needle, he would spare no pains to make *Heloise* answer the hopes which her uncle had conceived of her.

The canon was transported with the civility of the young doctor; he returned him thanks, and protested he could not do him a more acceptable service than to assist his niece in her endeavours to learn; he therefore entreated him once more to set apart some of his time, which he did not employ in public, for this purpose: and, (as if he had known his designed intrigue, and was willing to promote it) he committed her entirely to his care, and begged of him to treat her with the authority of a master; not only to chide her, but even to correct her whenever she was guilty of any neglect or disobedience to his commands.

Fulbert, in this, showed a simplicity without example but the affection which he had for his niece was so blind, and *Abelard* had so well established his reputation for wisdom, that the uncle never scrupled in the least to trust them together, and thought he had all the security in the world for their virtue. *Abelard* you may be sure, made use of the freedom which was given him. He saw his beautiful creature every hour, he set her lessons every day, and was extremely pleased to see what proficiency she made. *Heloise*, for her part, was so taken with her master, that she liked nothing so well as what she learned from him; and the master was charmed with that quickness of apprehension with which his scholar learned the most difficult lessons. But he did not intend to stop here. He knew so well how to insinuate into the affections of this young person, he gave her such plain intimations of what was in his heart and spoke so agreeably of the passion which he had conceived for her, that he had the satisfaction of seeing himself well understood. It is no difficult matter to make a girl of eighteen in love; and *Abelard* having so much wit and agreeable humour, must needs make a greater progress in her affections than she did in the lessons which he taught her; so that in a short time she fell so much in love with him, that she could deny him nothing.

Fulbert had a country-house at Corbeil, to which the lovers often resorted, under pretence of applying themselves more closely to their studies: there they conversed freely and gave themselves up entirely to the pleasure of a mutual passion. They took advantage of that privacy which study and contemplation require without subjecting themselves to the censure of those who observed it.

In this retirement *Abelard* owns that more time was employ'd in soft caresses than in lectures of philosophy. Sometimes he pretended to use the severity of a master; the better to deceive such as might be spies upon them, he exclaimed against *Heloise*, and reproached her for her negligence. But how different were his menaces from those which are inspired by anger!

Never did two lovers give a greater loose to their delights than did these two for five or six months; they lived in all the endearments which could enter into the hearts of young beginners. This is *Abelard's* own account of the matter. He compares himself to such as have been long kept in a starving condition, and at last are brought to a feast. A grave and studious man exceeds a debauchee in his enjoyments of a woman whom he loves and of whom he is passionately beloved.

Abelard being thus enchanted with the caresses of his mistress, neglected all his serious and important affairs. His performances in public were wretched. His scholars perceived it, and soon guessed the reason. His head was turned to nothing but amorous verses. His school was his aversion, and he spent as little time in it as he could. As for his lectures they were commonly the old ones served up again: the night was wholly lost from his studies; and his leisure was employed in writing songs, which were dispersed and sung in diverse provinces of France many years after. In short our lovers, who were in their own opinion the happiest pair in the world, kept so little guard, that their amours were every where talked of, and all the world saw plainly that the sciences were not always the subject of their conversation. Only honest Fulbert, under whose nose all this was done, was the last man that heard any thing of it; he wanted eyes to see that which was visible to all the world; and if any body went about to tell him of it, he was prepossessed with so good an opinion of his niece and her master, that he would believe nothing against them.

But at last so many discoveries were daily made to him, that he could not help believing something; he therefore resolved to separate them, and by that means prevent the ill consequences of their too great familiarity. However, he thought it best to convict them himself, before he proceeded further; and therefore watched them so closely, that he had one day an opportunity of receiving ocular satisfaction that the reports he had heard were true. In short he surprised them together. And though he was naturally cholerick, yet he appeared so moderate on this occasion as to leave them under dismal apprehensions of something worse to come after. The result was, that they must be parted.

Who can express the torment our lovers felt upon this separation! However, it served only to unite their hearts more firmly; they were but the more eager to see one another. Difficulties increased their desires, and put them upon any attempts without regarding what might be the consequence. *Abelard* finding it impossible to live without his dear *Heloise*, endeavoured to settle a correspondence with her by her maid Agaton, who was a handsome brown girl, well shaped, and likely enough to have pleased a man who was not otherwise engaged. But what a surprise was it to our Doctor, to find this girl refuse his money, and in recompence of the services she was to do him with his mistress, demanded no less a reward than his heart, and making him at once a plain declaration of love! *Abelard* who could love none but *Heloise*, turned from her abruptly, without answering a word. But a rejected woman is a dangerous creature. Agaton knew well how to revenge the affront put upon her, and failed not to acquaint Fulbert with *Abelard's* offers to her, without saying a word how she had been disobliged. Fulbert thought it was time to look about him. He thanked the maid for her care, and entered into measures with her, how to keep *Abelard* from visiting his niece.

The Doctor was now more perplexed than ever: he had no ways left but to apply himself to *Heloise's* singing-master; and the gold which the maid refused prevailed with him. By this means *Abelard* conveyed a letter to *Heloise*, in which he told her, that he intended to come and see her at night, and that the way he had contrived was over the garden-wall by a ladder of cords. This project succeeded, and brought them together. After the first transports of this short interview, *Heloise*, who had found some more than ordinary symptoms within her, acquainted her lover with it. She had informed him of it before by a letter; and now having this opportunity to consult about it; they agreed that she should go to a sister of his in Britany, at whose house she might be privately brought to bed. But before they parted, he endeavored to comfort her, and make her easy in this distress, by giving her assurances of marriage. When *Heloise* heard this proposal she peremptorily rejected it, and gave such reasons[5] for her refusal, as left *Abelard* in the greatest astonishment.

Indeed a refusal of this nature is so extraordinary a thing, that perhaps another instance of it is not to be found in history. I persuade myself, therefore, that I shall not offend my reader, if I make some few remarks upon it. It often happens, that the passion of love stifles or over-rules the rebukes of conscience; but it is unusual for it to extinguish the sensibility of honour. I don't speak of persons of mean birth and no education; but for others, all young women, I suppose, who engage in love-intrigues, flatter themselves with one of these views; either they hope they shall not prove with child, or they shall conceal it from the world, or they shall get themselves married. As for such as resolve to destroy the fruit of their amours, there are but few so void of all natural affections as to be capable of this greatest degree of barbarity. However, this shows plainly, that if Love tyrannizes sometimes, it is such a tyrant as leaves honour in possession of its rights. But *Heloise* had a passion so strong, that she was not at all

---

[5] See *Abelard's* letter to *Philintus*, and *Heloise's* first *Letter to Abelard*.

concerned for her honour or reputation. She was overjoyed to find herself with child, and yet she did her utmost not to be married. Never fore was so odd an example as these two things made when put together. The first was very extraordinary; and how many young women in the world would rather be married to a disagreeable husband than live in a state of reproach? They know the remedy is bad enough, and will cost them dear; but what signifies that, so long as the name of husband hides the flaws made in their honour? But as for *Heloise*, she was not so nice in this point. An excess of passion, never heard of before, made her chuse to be *Abelard's* mistress rather than his wife. We shall see, in the course of this history, how firm she was in this resolution, with what arguments she supported it, and how earnestly she persuaded her gallant to be of the same mind.

Abelard, who was willing to lose no time, least his dear *Heloise* should fall into her uncle's hands, disguised her in the habit of a nun, and sent her away with the greatest dispatch, hoping that after she was brought to bed, he should have more leisure to persuade her to marriage, by which they might screen themselves from the reproach which must otherwise come upon them, as soon as the business should be publickly known.

As soon as *Heloise* was set forward on her journey, *Abelard* resolved to make Fulbert a visit in order to appease him, if possible, and prevent the ill effects of his just indignation.

The news that *Heloise* was privately withdrawn soon made a great noise in the neighbourhood; and reaching Fulbert's ears, filled him with grief and melancholy. Besides, that he had a very tender affection for his niece, and could not live without her, he had the utmost resentment of the affront which *Abelard* had put upon him, by abusing the freedom he had allowed him. This fired him with such implacable fury, as in the end fell heavy upon our poor lovers, and had very dreadful consequences.

When Fulbert saw *Abelard*, and heard from him the reason why *Heloise* was withdrawn, never was man in such a passion. He abandoned himself to the utmost distractions of rage, despair, and thirst of revenge. All the affronts, reproaches, and menaces that could be thought of, were heaped upon *Abelard*; who was, poor man, very passive, and ready to make the Canon all the satisfaction he was able.

He gave him leave to say what he pleased; and when he saw that he tired himself with exclaiming, he took up the discourse, and ingenuously confess'd his crime. Then he had recourse to all the prayers, submissions, and promises, he could invent; and begged of him to consider the force of Love, and what foils this tyrant has given to the greatest men: that the occasion of the present misfortunes was the most violent passion that ever was; that this passion continued still; and that he was ready to give both him and his niece all the satisfaction which this sort of injury required. Will you marry her then? said Fulbert, interrupting him. Yes, replied *Abelard*, if you please, and she will consent. If I please! said the Canon, pausing a little; if she will consent! And do you question either? Upon this he was going to offer him his reasons, after his hasty way, why they should be married: But *Abelard* entreated him to suppress his passion a while, and hear what he had to offer: which was, that their marriage might for some time be kept secret. No, says the Canon, the dishonor you have done my niece is public, and the reparation you make her shall be so too, But *Abelard* told him, that since they were to be one family, he hoped he would consider his interest as his own. At last after a great many intreaties, Fulbert seemed content it should be as *Abelard* desired; that he should marry *Heloise* after she was brought to bed, and that in the mean time the business should be kept secret.

Abelard, having given his scholars a vacation, returned into Britany to visit his designed spouse, and to acquaint her with what had passed. She was not at all concerned at her uncle's displeasure; but that which troubled her was, the resolution which she saw her lover had taken to marry her, She endeavoured to dissuade him from it with all the arguments she could think of. She begun with representing to him the wrong he did himself in thinking of marriage: that as she never loved him but for his own sake, she preferred his glory, reputation, and interest, before her own. I know my uncle, said she, will never be pacified with any thing we can do, and what honour shall I get by being your wife, when at the same time I certainly ruin your reputation? What curse may I not justly fear, should I rob the world of so eminent a person as you are? What an injury shall I do the Church? how much shall I disoblige the learned? and what a shame and disparagement will it be to you, whom Nature has fitted for the public good, to devote yourself entirely to a wife? Remember what St. *Paul* says, *Art thou loosed from a wife? seek not a wife.* If neither this great man, not the fathers of the church, can make you change your resolution, consider at least what your philosophers say of it. Socrates

~ 14 ~

has proved, by many arguments, that a wife man ought not to marry. Tully put away his wife Terentia; and when Hircius offered him his sister in marriage he told him, he desired to be excused, because he could never bring himself to divide his thoughts between his books and his wife. In short, said she, how can the study of divinity and philosophy comport with the cries of children, the songs of nurses, and all the hurry of a family? What an odd fight will it be to see maids and scholars, desks and cradles, books and distaffs, pens and spindles, one among another? Those who are rich are never disturbed with the care and charges of housekeeping; but with you scholars it is far otherwise[6].

He that will get an estate must mind the affairs of the world, and consequently is taken off from the study of divinity and philosophy. Observe the conduct of the wife Pagans in this point, who preferred a single life before marriage, and be ashamed that you cannot come up to them. Be more careful to maintain the character and dignity of a philosopher. Don't you know, that there is no action of life which draws after it so sure and long a repentance, and to so little purpose? You fancy to yourself the enjoyments you shall have in being bound to me by a bond which nothing but death can break: but know there is no such thing as sweet chains; and there is a thousand times more glory, honour, and pleasure, in keeping firm to an union which love alone has established, which is supported by mutual esteem and merit, and which owes its continuance to nothing but the satisfaction of seeing each other free. Shall the laws and customs which the gross and carnal world has invented hold us together more surely than the bonds of mutual affection? Take my word for it, you'll see me too often when you see me ev'ry day: you'll have no value for my love nor favours when they are due to you, and cost you no care. Perhaps you don't think of all this at present; but you'll think of nothing else when it will be too late. I don't take notice what the world will say, to see a man in your circumstances get him a wife, and so throw away your reputation, your fortune and your quiet. In short, continued she, the quality of mistress is a hundred times more pleasing to me than that of a wife. Custom indeed, has given a dignity to this latter name, and we are imposed upon by it; but Heaven is my witness, I had rather be *Abelard's* mistress than lawful wife to the Emperor of the whole world. I am very sure I shall always prefer your advantage and

---

[6] *Heloissa dehortabat me nuptiis. Nuptia non conveniunt cum philosophia*, &c. Oper. Abel. p 14.

satisfaction before my own honour, and all the reputation, wealth, and enjoyments, which the most splendid marriage could bring me. Thus *Heloise* argued, and added a great many more reasons, which I forbear to relate, lest I should tire my reader. It is enough for him to know, that they are chiefly grounded upon her preference of love to marriage, and liberty to necessity.

We might therefore suppose that *Heloise* was afraid lest marriage should prove the tomb of love. The Count de Buffi, who passes for the translator of some of her Letters, makes this to be her meaning, though cloathed in delicate language. But if we examine those which she writ to *Abelard* after their separation, and the expressions she uses to put him in mind, that he was indebted for the passion she had for him to nothing but love itself, we must allow that she had more refined notions, and that never woman was so disinterested. She loved *Abelard* 'tis true; but she declared it was not his sex that she most valued in him.

Some authors[7] are of opinion, that it was not an excess of love which made *Abelard* press *Heloise* to marriage, but only to quiet his conscience: but how can any one tell his reasons for marriage better than he himself? Others say[8] that if *Heloise* did really oppose *Abelard's* design of marrying her so earnestly, it was not because she thought better of concubinage than a married life, but because her affection and respect for her lover leading her to seek his honour and advantage in all things, she was afraid that by marrying him she should stand between him and a bishoprick, which his wit and learning well deserved. But there is no such thing in her Letters, nor in the long account which *Abelard* has left us of the arguments which his mistress used to dissuade him from marriage. These are the faults of many authors, who put such words in the mouths of persons as are most conformable to their own ideas. It is often more advantageous, that a woman should leave her lover free for church dignities, than render him incapable of them by marriage: but is it just therefore to suppose that *Heloise* had any such motives? There is indeed a known story of a man that was possessed of a prebend, and quitted it for a wife. The day after the wedding, he said to his bride, My dear, consider how passionately I loved you, since I lost my preferment to

---

[7] *D'ctionnaire de Moreri*
[8] *Fran. d'Amboise.*

~ 16 ~

marry you. You have done a very foolish thing, said she; you might have kept that, and have had me notwithstanding.

But to return to our lovers. A modern author, who well understood human nature, has affirmed, "That women by the favours they grant to men, grow she fonder of them; but, on the contrary, the men grow more indifferent."[9] This is not always true, *Abelard* was not the less enamoured with *Heloise* after she had given him the utmost proofs of her love; and their familiarity was so far from having abated his flame, that it seems all the eloquence of *Heloise* could not persuade *Abelard* that he wronged himself in thinking to marry her. He admired the wit, the passion, and the ingenuity of his mistress, but in these things he did not come short of her. He knew so well how to represent to her the necessity of marriage, the discourse which he had about it with Fulbert, his rage if they declined it, and how dangerous it might be to both of them, that at last she consented to do whatever he pleased: but still with an inconceivable reluctance, which showed that she yielded for no other reason but the fear of disobliging him.

Abelard was willing to be near his mistress till she was brought to bed, which in a short time she was of a boy. As soon as *Heloise* was fit to go abroad, *Abelard* carried her to Paris, where they were married in the most private manner that could be, having no other company but Fulbert, and two or three particular friends. However, the wedding quickly came to be known. The news of it was already whispered about; people soon began to talk of it more openly, till at last they mentioned it to the married pair.

Fulbert who was less concerned to keep his word than to cover the reproach of his family, took care to spread it abroad. But *Heloise*, who loved *Abelard* a thousand times better than she did herself, and always valued her dear Doctor's honour above her own, denied it with the most solemn protestations, and did all she could to make the world believe her. She constantly affirmed, that the reports of it were mere slanders; that *Abelard* never proposed any such thing; and if he had, she would never have consented to it. In short, she denied it so constantly, and with such earnestness, that she was generally believed. Many people thought, and boldly affirmed, that the Doctor's enemies had spread this story on purpose to lessen his character. This report came to Fulbert's ears, who, knowing that *Heloise* was the sole

---

[9] *M. de la Bruyere.*

author of it, fell into so outrageous a passion at her, that after a thousand reproaches and menaces, he proceeded to use her barbarously. But *Abelard*, who loved her never the worse for being his wife, could not see this many days with patience. He resolved therefore to order matters so as to deliver her from this state of persecution. To this purpose they consulted together what course was to be taken; and agreed, that for setting them both free, her from the power and ill-humour of her uncle, and him from the persecuting reports which went about of him, *Heloise* should retire into a convent, where she should take the habit of a nun, all but the veil, that so she might easily come out again, when they should have a more favourable opportunity. This design was proposed, approved, and executed, almost at the same time. By this means they effectually put a stop to all reports about a marriage. But the Canon was too dangerous a person to be admitted to this consultation; he would never have agreed to their proposal; nor could he hear of it without the utmost rage. 'Twas then that he conceived a new desire of revenge, which he pursued till he had executed it in the most cruel manner imaginable. This retreat of *Heloise* gave him the more sensible affliction, because she was so far from covering her own reputation, that she completed his shame. He considered it as *Abelard*'s contrivance, and a fresh instance of his perfidious dealing towards him. And this reflection put him upon studying how to be revenged on them both at one stroke; which, aiming at the root of the mischief, should forever disable them from offending again.

While this plot was in agitation, the lovers, who were not apt to trouble their heads about what might happen, spent their time in the most agreeable manner that could be. *Abelard* could not live long without a sight of his dear wife. He made her frequent visits in the convent of Argenteuil, to which she was retired. The nuns of this abbey enjoyed a very free kind of life: the grates and parlours were open enough. As for *Heloise*, she had such excellent qualifications as made the good sisters very fond of her, and extremely pleased that they had such an amiable companion. And as they were not ignorant what reports there were abroad, that she was married to the famous *Abelard*, (though she denied it to the last,) the most discerning among them, observing the frequent visits of the Doctor, easily imagined that she had reasons for keeping herself private, and so they took her case into consideration, and expressed a wonderful compassion for her misfortunes.

Some of them, whom *Heloise* loved above the rest, and in whom she put great confidence, were not a little aiding and assisting in the private interviews which she had with *Abelard*, and in giving him opportunities to enter the convent. The amorous Doctor made the best use of every thing. The habit which *Heloise* wore the place where he was to see her, the time and seasons proper for his visit, the stratagems which must be used to facilitate his entrance, and carry him undiscovered to *Heloise's* chamber, the difficulties they met with, the reasons they had for not letting it be known who they were, and the fear they were in of being taken together; all this gave their amours an air of novelty, and added to their lawful embraces all the taste of stolen delights.

These excesses had then their charms, but in the end had fatal consequences. The furious Canon persisting in his design of being revenged on *Abelard*, notwithstanding his marriage with his niece, found means to corrupt a domestic of the unfortunate Doctor, who gave admittance into his master's chamber to some assassins hired by Fulbert, who seized him in his sleep, and cruelly deprived him of his manhood, but not his life. The servant and his accomplices fled for it. The wretched *Abelard* raised such terrible outcries, that the people in the house and the neighbours being alarmed, hastened to him, and gave such speedy assistance, that he was soon out of a condition of fearing death.

The news of this accident made great noise, and its singularity raised the curiosity of abundance of persons, who came the next day as in procession, to see, to lament and comfort him. His scholars loudly bewailed his misfortune, and the women distinguished themselves upon this occasion by extraordinary marks of tenderness. And 'tis probable among the great number of ladies who pitied *Abelard*, there were some with whom he had been very intimate: for his philosophy did not make him scrupulous enough to esteem every small infidelity a crime, when it did not lessen his constant love of *Heloise*.

This action of Fulbert was too tragical to pass unpunished: the traiterous servant and one of the assassins were seized and condemned to lose their eyes, and to suffer what they had done to *Abelard*. But Fulbert denying he had any share in the action saved himself from the punishment with the loss only of his benefices. This sentence did not satisfy *Abelard*; he made his complaint to no purpose to the bishop and canons; and if he had made a remonstrance at Rome, where he once had a design of carrying the matter, 'tis probable he would have had no better success. It requires too much money to gain a cause there. One *Foulques*, prior of Deuil, and intimate friend of *Abelard*, wrote thus to him upon the occasion of his misfortune: "If you appeal to the Pope without bringing an immense sum of money, it will be useless: nothing can satisfy the infinite avarice and luxury of the Romans. I question if you have enough for such an undertaking; and if you attempt it, nothing will perhaps remain but the vexation of having flung away so much money. They who go to Rome without large sums to squander away, will return just as they went, the expence of their journey only excepted."[10] But since I am upon Foulques's letters which is too extraordinary to be passed over in silence, I shall give the reader some reflections which may make him amends for the trouble of a new digression.

This friend of *Abelard* lays before him many advantages which might be drawn from his misfortune. He tells him his extraordinary talents, subtilty, eloquence and learning had drawn from all parts an incredible number of auditors, and so filled him with excessive vanity: he hints gently at another thing, which contributed not a little towards making him proud, namely, that the women continually followed him, and gloried in drawing him into their snares. This misfortune, therefore, would cure him of his pride, and free him from those snares of women which had reduced him even to indigence, tho' his profession got him a large revenue; and now he would never impoverish himself by his gallantries.

Heloise herself, in some passages of her *Letters*, says, that there was neither maid nor wife,[11] who in *Abelard's* absence did not form designs for him, and in his presence was not inflamed with love: the queens themselves, and ladies of the first quality, envied the pleasures she enjoyed with him. But we are not to take these words of *Heloise* in a strict sense; because as she loved *Abelard* to madness, so she imagined every one else did. Besides, that report, to be sure, hath added to the truth. It is not at all probable that a man of *Abelard's* sense, and who according to all appearance passionately loved his

---

[10] *This Letter is extant in* Latin *in* Abelard's *Works*.
[11] *Qua conjugata, que virgo non concupiscebat absentem, & non exardescebat in presentem? Qua regina, vel prapotens foemina gaudiis meis non invidebat, vel thalamis?*

wife, should not be able to contain himself within some bounds, but should squander away all his money upon mistresses, even to his not reserving what was sufficient to provide for his necessities. Foulques owns, that he speaks only upon hearsay, and in that, no doubt, envy, and jealousy had their part.

Foulques tells him besides, that the amputation of a part of his body, of which he made such ill use, would suppress at the same time a great many troublesome passions, and procure him liberty of reflecting on himself, instead of being hurried to and fro by his passions: his meditations would be no more interrupted by the emotions of the flesh, and therefore he would be more successful in discovering the secrets of Nature. He reckons it as a great advantage to him, that he would no more be the terror of husbands, and might now lodge any where without being suspected. And forgets not to acquaint him, that he might converse with the finest women without any fear of those temptations which sometimes overpower even age itself upon the sight of such objects. And, lastly, he would have the happiness of being exempt from the illusions of sleep; which exemption, according to him is a peculiar blessing.

It was with reason that Foulques reckons all these as advantages very extraordinary in the life of an ecclesiastick. It is easy to observe, that, to a person who devotes himself to continence, nothing can be more happy than to be insensible to beauty and love, for they who cannot maintain their chastity but by continual combats are very unhappy. The life of such persons is uneasy, their state always doubtful. They but too much feel the trouble of their warfare; and if they come off victorious in an engagement, it is often with a great many wounds. Even such of them as in a retired life are at the greatest distance from temptations, by continually struggling with their inclinations, setting barriers against the irruptions of the flesh, are in a miserable condition. Their entrenchments are often forced, and their conscience filled with sorrow and anxiety. What progress might one make in the ways of virtue, who is not obliged to fight an enemy for every foot of ground? Had *Abelard's* misfortune made him indeed such as Foulques supposed, we should see him in his *Letters* express his motives of comfort with a better grace. But though he now was in a condition not able to satisfy a passion by which he had suffered so much, yet was he not insensible at the sight of those objects which once gave him so much pleasure. This discourse therefore of

Pierre Abelard

Foulques, far from comforting *Abelard* in his affliction, seems capable of producing the contrary effect; and it is astonishing if *Abelard* did not take it so, and think he rather insulted him, and consequently resent it.

As to dreams, St. Austin informs us of the advantage Foulques tells his friend he had gained. St. Austin implores the grace of God to deliver him from this sort of weakness, and says, he gave consent to those things in his sleep which he should abominate awake, and laments exceedingly so great a regaining weakness.

But let us go on with this charitable friend's letter; it hath too near a relation to this to leave any part of it untouched. Matrimonial functions (continues Foulques) and the cares of a family, will not now hinder your application to please God. And what a happiness is it, not to be in a capacity of sinning? And then he brings the examples of Origen, and other martyrs, who rejoice now in heaven for their being upon earth in the condition *Abelard* laments; as if the impossibility of committing a sin could secure any one from desiring to do it. But one of the greatest motives of comfort, and one upon which he insists the most is, because his misfortune is irreparable. This is indeed true in fact, but the consequence of his reasoning is not so certain; *Afflict not yourself* (says he) *because your misfortune is of such a nature as is never to be repaired.*

It must be owned, that the general topics of consolation have two faces, and may therefore be considered very differently, even so as to seem arguments for sorrow. As for instance, one might argue very justly, that a mother should not yield too much to grief upon the loss of a son, because her tears are unavailable; and tho' she should kill herself with sorrow, she can never, by these means, bring her son to life. Yet this very thing, that all she can do is useless, is the main occasion of her grief; she could bear it patiently, could she any ways retrieve her loss. When Solon lamented the death of his son, and some friend, by way of comfort, told him his tears were insignificant. *That,* said he, *is the very reason why I weep.*

But Foulques argues much better afterwards; he says, *Abelard* did not suffer this in the commission of an ill act, but sleeping peaceably in his bed; that is he was not caught in any open fact, such has cost others the like loss. This is indeed a much better topic than the former, though it must be allowed that *Abelard* had drawn this misfortune on himself by a crime as bad as adultery; yet the fault was over, and he had made all the reparation in his power, and when they maimed him he thought no harm to any body.

Abelard's friend makes use likewise of other consolatory reasons in his Letter, and represents to him, after a very moving manner, the part which the Bishop and Canons, and all the Ecclesiasticks of Paris, took in his disgrace, and the mourning there was among the inhabitants and especially the women, upon this occasion. But, in this article of consolation, how comes it to pass that he makes no mention of *Heloise*? This ought not to appear strange: she was the most injured, and therefore questionless, her sorrows were sufficiently known to him; and it would be no news to tell the husband that his wife was in the utmost affliction for him. For as we observed before, though she was in a convent, she had not renounced her husband, and those frequent visits he made her were not spent in reading homilies. But let us make an end of our reflections on Foulques's curious Letter, Foulques, after advising *Abelard* not to think of carrying the matter before the Pope, by assuring him that it required too great expence to obtain any satisfaction at that court, concludes all with this last motive of consolation, that the imagined happiness he had lost was always accompanied with abundance of vexation; but if he persevered in his spirit of resignation, he would, without doubt, at the last day obtain that justice he had now failed of. 'Tis great pity we have not *Abelard's* answer to this delicate Letter, the matter then would look like one of Job's Dialogues with his friends. *Abelard* would generally have enough to reply, and Foulques would often be but a sorry comforter. However, it is certain this Letter was of some weight with *Abelard*; for we find afterwards he never thought of making a voyage to Rome. Resolved to hear his calamity patiently, he left to God the avenging of the cruel and shameful abuse he had suffered.

But let us return to *Heloise*. 'Tis probable her friends of the convent of Argenteuil concealed so heavy a misfortune from her for some time; but at last she heard the fatal news. Though the rage and fury of her uncle threatened her long since with some punishment, yet could she never suspect any thing of this nature. It will be saying too little to tell the reader she felt all the shame and sorrow that is possible. She only can express those violent emotions of her soul upon so severe an occasion.

Pierre Abelard

In all probability this misfortune of *Abelard* would have been a thorough cure of her passion, if we might argue from like cases: but there is no rule so general as not to admit of some exceptions; and *Heloise's* love upon this severe trial proved like Queen Stratonice's, who was not less passionate for her favourite Combabus, when she discovered his impotence, than she had been before.

Shame and sorrow had not less seized *Abelard* than *Heloise*, nor dared he ever appear in the world; so that he resolved, immediately upon his cure, to banish himself from the sight of men, and hide himself in the darkness of a monastick life avoiding all conversation with any kind of persons excepting his dear *Heloise*, by whose company he endeavoured to comfort himself. But she at last resolved to follow his example, and continue forever in the convent of Argenteuil where she was. *Abelard* himself confesses, that shame rather than devotion had made him take the habit of a monk; and that it was jealousy more than love which engaged him to persuade *Heloise* to be professed before he had made his vow. The Letters which follow this history will inform us after what manner and with what resolution they separated. *Heloise* in the twenty-second year of her age generously quitted the world, and renounced all those pleasures she might reasonably have promised herself, to sacrifice herself entirely to the fidelity and obedience she owed her husband, and to procure him that ease of mind which he said he could no otherwise hope for.

Time making *Abelard's* misfortune familiar to him, he now entertained thoughts of ambition, and of supporting the reputation he had gained of the most learned man of the age. He began with explaining the *Acts of the Apostles* to the monks of the monastery of St. *Dennis* to which he had retired; but the disorders of the abbey, and debauchees of the Abbot, which equally with his dignity, were superior to those of the simple monks, quickly drove him hence. He had made himself uneasy to them by censuring their irregularity. They were glad to part with him, and he to leave them.

As soon as he had obtained leave of the Abbot, he retired to Thinbaud in Champaign, where he set up a school, persuading himself that his reputation would bring him a great number of scholars. And indeed they flocked to him, not only from the most distant provinces of Prance, but also from Rome, Spain, England, and

Germany, in such number, that the towns could not provide accommodation, nor the country provisions, enough for them,[12] But *Abelard* did not foresee, that this success and reputation would at the same time occasion him new troubles. He had made himself two considerable enemies at Laon, Alberic of Rheims, and Lotulf of Lombardy, who, as soon as they perceived how prejudicial his reputation was to their schools, sought all occasions to ruin him; and thought they had a lucky handle to do so from a book of his, intituled, *The Mystery of the Trinity*. This they pretended was heretical, and through the Archbishop's means they procured a council at Soissons in the year 1121; and without suffering *Abelard* to make any defence, ordered his book to be burnt by his own hands, and himself to be confined to the convent of St. Medard. This sentence gave him such grief, that he says himself, the unhappy fate of his writing touched him more sensibly than the misfortune he had suffered through Fulbert's means. Nor was it only his fatherly concern for his own productions, but the indelible mark of heresy which by this means was fixed on him, which so exceedingly troubled him.

That the curious reader may have a complete knowledge of this matter, I shall here give an account of that pretended heresy which was imputed to *Abelard*. The occasion of his writing this book was, that his scholars demanded[13] philosophical arguments on that subject; often urging that it was impossible to believe what was not understood; that it was to abuse the world, to preach a doctrine equally unintelligible to the speaker and auditor; and that it was for the blind to lead the blind. These young men were certainly inclined to Sabellinism. *Abelard's* enemies however did not accuse him of falling into this, but another heresy as bad, Tritheism; though indeed he was equally free from both: he explained the unity of the Godhead by comparisons drawn from human things but according to a passage of St. Bernard,[14] one of his greatest enemies, he seemed to hold, that no one ought to believe what he could not give a reason for. However *Abelard's* treatise upon this subject pleased every one except those of his own profession, who, stung with envy that he should find out explanations which they could not have thought of, raised such a cry of heresy upon him, that he and some of his scholars had like to have

---

[12] *Ad quas scholas tanta scholarium multitudo confluxit ut nec locus hospitiis, nec terra sufficeret alimentis.* Abel. Oper. p. 19
[13] *Humanas & philosophicas rationes requirebant. & plus quae inteligi, quam quae dici poffenter, efflagitabant.* Abel Op.
[14] *Benardi Epist.* 190.

been stoned by the mob.[15] By their powerful cabals they prevailed with Conan bishop of Preneste, the Pope's legate, who was president of the council, to condemn his book, pretending that he asserted three Gods, which they might easily suggest, when he was suffered to make no defence. 'Tis certain he was very orthodox in the doctrine of the Trinity; and all this process against him was only occasioned by the malice of his enemies. His logical comparison (and logic was his masterpiece) proved rather the three Divine Persons One, than multiplied the Divine Nature into Three. His comparison is, that as the three proportions[16] in a syllogism are but one truth, so the Father, Son, and Holy Ghost, are but one Essence; and it is certain the inconveniences which may be drawn from this parallel are not more than what may be drawn from the comparison of the three dimensions of solids, so much insisted on by the famous orthodox mathematician Dr. Wallis of England. But great numbers of pious and learned divines, who have not been over-subtile in politics, have been persecuted and condemned as well as *Abelard* by the ignorance and malice of their brethren.

A little after his condemnation, *Abelard* was ordered to return to St. Dennis. The liberty he had taken to censure the vicious lives of the monks had raised him a great many enemies. Amongst these was St. Bernard, not upon the same motives as those monks, but because *Abelard's* great wit, joined with so loose and sensual a life, gave him jealousy, who thought it impossible the heart should be defiled without the head being likewise tainted.

Scarce had he returned to St. Dennis, when one day he dropped some words, intimating he did not believe that the St. Dennis their patron was the Areopagite mentioned in the Scripture, there being no probability that he ever was in France. This was immediately carried to the Abbot, who was full of joy, that he had now a handle to heighten the accusations of heresy against him with some crime against the state; a method frequently used by this sort of gentlemen to make sure their revenge. In those times, too, the contradicting the notions of the monks was enough to prove a man an atheist, heretic, rebel, or any thing; learning signified nothing. If any one of a clearer

---

[15] *Ita me in clero & populo diffamaverunt, ut pene me populos paucosque qui advenerant ex discipulis nostris prima die nostri anventus lapidarent; dicentes me tres Deos praedicare & scripsisse, sicut ipsis persuasum fuerat.* Abel Oper. p. 20.
[16] *Sicut eadem oratio est, propositio, assumptio & conuclusio, ita eadem Essentia est Pater, Filius, and Spiritus Sanctis.* Ibid.

head and larger capacity had the misfortune to be suspected of novelty, there was no way to avoid the general persecution of the monks but voluntarily banishing himself. The Abbot immediately assembled all the house, and declared he would deliver up to the secular power a person who had dared to reflect upon the honour of the kingdom and of the crown. *Abelard* very rightly judging that such threatenings were not to be despised, fled by night to Champaign, to a cloister of the monks of Troies, and there patiently waited till the storm should be over. After the death of this Abbot, which, very luckily for him happened soon after his flight, he obtained leave to live where he pleased, though it was not without using some cunning. He knew the monks of so rich a house had fallen into great excesses, and were very obnoxious to the court, who would not fail to make their profit of it: he therefore procured it should be represented to his council as very disadvantageous to his Majesty's interest, that a person who was continually censuring the lives of his brethren should continue any longer with them. This was immediately understood, and orders given to some great men at court to demand of the Abbot and monks why they kept a person in their house whose conduct was so disagreeable to them; and, far from being an ornament to the society, was a continual vexation, by publishing their faults? This being very opportunely moved to the new Abbot, he gave *Abelard* leave to retire to what cloister he pleased.

Abelard, who indeed had all the qualities which make a great man, could not however bear, without repining, the numerous misfortunes with which he saw himself embarrassed, and had frequent thoughts of publishing a manifesto to justify himself from the scandalous imputations his enemies had laid upon him and to undeceive those whom their malice had prejudiced against him. But upon cooler thought he determined, that it was better to say nothing and to shew them by his silence how unworthy he thought them of his anger. Thus being rather enraged than troubled at the injuries he had suffered, he resolved to found a new society, consisting chiefly of monks. To this purpose he chose a solitude in the diocese of Troies, and upon some ground which was given by permission of the Bishop, he built a little house and a chapel, which he dedicated to the most Holy Trinity.

Men of learning were then scarce, and the desire of science was beginning to spread itself. Our exile was inquired after and found;

scholars crowded to him from all parts: they built little huts, and were very liberal to their master for his lectures; content to live on herbs, and roots, and water, that they might have the advantage of learning from so extraordinary a man; and with great zeal they enlarged the chapel building that and their professor's house with wood and stone.

Upon this occasion *Abelard*, to continue the memory of the comfort he had received in this desert, dedicated his new built chapel to the Holy Ghost, by the name of the Paraclete, or Comforter. The envy of Alberic and Lotulf, which had long since persecuted him, was strangely revived, upon seeing so many scholars flock to him from all parts, notwithstanding the inconvenience of the place, and in contempt of the masters who might so commodiously be found in the towns and cities.

They now more than ever sought occasion to trouble him; the name of Paraclete furnished them with one. They gave out that this novelty was a consequence of his former heresy, and that it was no more lawful to dedicate churches to the Holy Ghost than to God the Father: that this title was a subtile art of instilling that poison which he durst not spread openly, and a consequence of his heretical doctrine which had been condemned already by a council. This report raised a great clamour among numbers of people, whom his enemies employed on all sides. But the persecution grew more terrible when St. Bernard and St. Norbet declared against him; two great zealots, fired with the spirit of Reformation, and who declared themselves restorers of the primitive discipline, and had wonderfully gained upon the affections of the populace. They spread such scandal against him that they prejudiced his principal friends, and forced those who still loved him not to shew it any ways; and upon these accounts made his life so bitter to him that he was upon the point of leaving Christendom.[17] But his unhappiness would not let him do a thing which might have procur'd his ease; but made him still continue with Christians, and with monks (as himself expresses it) worse than Heathens.[18]

---

[17] *Saepe autem (Deus scit) in tantam lapsus sum desperationem ut Christianorum finibus excessis, ad Gentes transire disponerem, atque ibi quiete sub quacunque tributi pactione inter inimicos Christi christiane vivere.* Abel Op. p. 32.
[18] *Incedi in Christianos atque monachos Gentibus longe saeviores atque pejores.* Abel Op. p. 20.

The Duke of Britany, informed of his misfortunes, and of the barbarity of his enemies, named him to the abbey of St. Gildas, in the diocese of Vannes, at the desire of the monks who had already elected him for their superior. Here he thought he had found a refuge from the rage of his enemies, but in reality he had only changed one trouble for another. The profligate lives of the monks, and the arbitrariness of a lord, who had deprived them of the greater part of their revenues, so that they were obliged to maintain their mistresses and children at their own private expence, occasioned him a thousand vexations and dangers. They several times endeavoured to poison him in his ordinary diet, but proving unsuccessful that way, they cried to do it in the holy sacrament. Excommunications, with which he threatened the most mutinous, did not abate the disorder. He now feared the poniard more than poison, and compared his case to his whom the tyrant of Saracuse caused to be seated at his table, with a sword hanging over him, fastened only by a thread.

Whilst *Abelard* thus suffered in his abbey by his monks, the nuns of Argenteuil, of whom *Heloise* was prioress, grew so licentious, that Sugger, abbot of Dennis, taking advantage of their irregularities, got possession of their monastery. He sent the original writings to Rome; and having obtained the answer he desired, he expelled the nuns, and established in their place monks of his order.

Some censorious people upon reading this passage, will be apt to entertain strong suspicions of *Heloise*, and judge it probable that a governor does not behave well when dissoluteness is known to reign in the society. I have never read that she was included by name in the general scandal of the society, and therefore am cautious not to bring any accusations against her. Our Saviour says, *No one hath condemned thee, neither do I condemn thee.*

Heloise, at her departure from the convent of Argenteuil, applied to her husband; who by permission of the Bishop Troies, gave her the house and chapel of the *Paraclete*, with its appendages; and placing there some nuns, founded a nunnery. Pope Innocent II. confirmed this donation in the year 1131. This is the origin of the abbey of the *Paraclete*, of which *Heloise* was the first abbess. Whatever her conduct was among the licentious nuns of Argenteuil, it is certain she lived so regular in this her new and last retreat, and behaved herself with that prudence, zeal, and piety, that she won the hearts of all the world, and in a small time had abundance of donations. *Abelard* himself says she had more in one year than he could have expected all his life, had he lived there. The bishops loved her as their child, the abbesses as their sister, and the world as their mother. It must be owned some women have had wonderful talents for exciting Christian charity. The abbesses which succeeded *Heloise* have often been of the greatest families in the kingdom. There is a list of them in the *Notes* of *Andrew du Chene* upon *Abelard's* works, from the time of the foundation in 1130, to 1615; but he has not thought fit to take notice of Jane Cabot, who died the 25th of June 1593, and professed the Protestant religion, yet without marrying, or quitting her habit, though she was driven from her abbey.

After *Abelard* had settled *Heloise* here, he made frequent journies from Britany to Champaign, to take care of the interest of this rising house, and to ease himself from the vexations of his own abbey. But slander so perpetually followed this unhappy man, that though his present condition was universally known, he was reproached with a remaining voluptuous passion for his former mistress. He complains of his hard usage in one of his Letters; but comforts himself by the example of St. Jerom, whose friendship with Paula occasioned scandal too; and therefore he entirely confuted this calumny, by remarking that even the most jealous commit their wives to the custody of eunuchs.

The thing which gives the greatest handle to suspect *Heloise's* prudence, and that *Abelard* did not think himself safe with her, is his making a resolution to separate himself forever from her. During his being employed in establishing this new nunnery, and in ordering their affairs, as well temporal as spiritual, he was diligent in persuading her, by frequent and pious admonitions, to such a separation; and insisted, that in order to make their retirement and penitence more profitable, it was absolutely necessary they should seriously endeavour to forget each other, and for the future think on nothing but God. When he had given her directions for her own conduct, and rules for the management of the nuns, he took his last leave of her and returned to his abbey in Britany where he continued a long time without her hearing any mention of him.

By chance, a letter he wrote to one of his friends, to comfort him under some disgrace, wherein he had given him a long account of all the persecutions he himself had suffered, fell into Heloise's hands. She knew by the superscription from whom it came, and her curiosity made her open it. The reading the particulars of a story she was so much concerned in renewed all her passion, and she hence took an occasion to write to him, complaining of his long silence. *Abelard* could not forbear answering her. This occasioned the several Letters between them which follow this History; and in these we may observe how high a woman is capable of railing the sentiments of her heart when possessed of a great deal of wit and learning, at well as a most violent love.

I shall not tire the reader with any farther reflections on the Letters of those two lovers, but leave them entirely to his own judgment; only remarking, that he ought not to be surprised to find *Heloise's* more tender, passionate, and expressive, than those of *Abelard*. She was younger and consequently more ardent than he. The sad condition he was in had not altered her love. Besides, she retired only in complaisance to a man she blindly yielded to; and resolving to preserve her fidelity inviolable, she strove to conquer her desires, and make a virtue of necessity. But the weakness of her sex continually returned, and she felt the force of love in spite of all resistance. It was not the same with *Abelard*; for though it was a mistake to think, that by not being in a condition of satisfying his passion, he was as *Heloise* imagined, wholly delivered from the thorn of sensuality; yet he was truly sorry for the disorders of his past life, he was sincerely penitent, and therefore his Letters are less violent and passionate than those of *Heloise*.

About ten years after *Abelard* had retired to his abbey, where study was his chief business, his enemies, who had resolved to persecute him to the last, were careful not to let him enjoy the ease of retirement. They thought he was not sufficiently plagued with his monks, and therefore brought a new process of heresy against him before the Archbishop of Sens. He desired he might have the liberty of defending his doctrine before a public assembly, and it was granted him. Upon this account the Council of Sens was assembled, in which Louis the VII, assisted in person, in the year 1140. St. Bernard was the accuser, and delivered to the assembly some propositions drawn from *Abelard's* book, which were read in the Council. This accusation gave *Abelard* such fears, and was managed with such inveterate malice by his enemies, and with such great unfairness, in drawing consequences he never thought of, that, imagining he had friends at Rome who would protect his innocence, he made an appeal to the Pope. The Council notwithstanding his appeal, condemned his book, but did not meddle with his person; and gave an account of the whole proceeding to Pope Innocent II. praying him to confirm their sentence. St. Bernard had been so early in prepossessing the Pontiff, that he got the sentence confirmed before *Abelard* heard any thing of it, or had any time to present himself before the tribunal to which he had appealed. His Holiness ordered besides, that *Abelard's* books should be burnt, himself confined, and for ever prohibited from teaching.

This passage of St. Bernard's life is not much for the honour of his memory: and whether he took the trouble himself to extract the condemned propositions from *Abelard's* works, or intrusted it to another hand, it is certain the paper he gave in contained many things which *Abelard* never wrote, and others which he did not mean in the same sense imputed to him.

When a few particular expressions are urged too rigidly, and unthought of consequences drawn from some assertions, and no regard is had to the general intent and scope of an author, it is no difficult matter to find errors in any book. For this reason, Beranger of Poitiers, *Abelard's* scholar defended his master against St. Bernard, telling him he ought not to persecute others, whose own writings were not exempt from errors; demonstrating, that he himself had advanced a position which he would not have failed to have inserted in this extract as a monstrous doctrine, if he had found them in the writings of *Abelard*.

Some time after *Abelard's* condemnation, the Pope was appeased at the solicitation of the Abbot of Clugni, who received this unfortunate gentleman into his monastery with great humanity, reconciled him with St. Bernard, and admitted him to be a Religious of his society.

This was *Abelard's* last retirement, in which he found all manner of kindness; he read lectures to the monks, and was equally humble and laborious. At last growing weak, and afflicted with a complication of diseases, he was sent to the priory of St. Marcel upon the Saone, near Chalons, a very agreeable place, where he died the

21st of April 1142, in the 63d year of his age. His corpse was sent to the chapel of *Paraclete*, to *Heloise*, to be interred, according to her former request of him, and to his own desire. The Abbot of Clugni, when he sent the body to *Heloise* according to the custom of those times, sent with it an absolution, to be fixed, together with his epitaph, on his grave-stone, which absolution was at follows:

"I Peter, Abbot of Clugni, having received Father *Abelard* into the number of my Religions, and given leave that his body be privately conveyed to the abbey of the Paraclete, to be disposed of by *Heloise* Abbess of the same abbey; do, by the authority of God and all the saints, absolve the said *Abelard* from all his sins."[19]

Heloise, who survived him twenty years, had all the leisure that could be to effect the cure of her unhappy passion. Alas! she was very long about it! she passed the rest of her days like a religions and devout Abbess, frequent in prayers, and entirely employed in the regulation of her society. She loved study; and being a mistress of the learned languages, the Latin, Greek, and Hebrew, she was esteemed a miracle of learning.

Abelard, in a letter he wrote to the Religious of his new house, says expressly, that *Heloise* understood these three languages. The Abbot of Clugni, likewise, in a letter he wrote to her, tells her, she excelled in learning not only all her sex, but the greatest part of men.[20] And in the calendar of the house of the Paraclete she is recorded in these words: *Heloise, mother and first abbess of this place, famous for her learning and religion.* I must not here pass by a custom the Religious of the *Paraclete* now have to commemorate how learned their first Abbess was in the Greek, which is, that every year, on the day of Pentecost, they perform divine service in the Greek tongue. What a ridiculous vanity!

Francis d'Amboise tells us how subtilely one day she satisfied St. Bernard, upon asking her, why in her abbey, when they recited the Lord's Prayer, they did not say, *Give us this day our* Daily *bread*, but *Give us this day our* Supersubstantial *bread*, by an argument drawn

---

[19] *Ego Petrus Cluniacensis Abbas, qui Pet. Abselardum in monacum Cluniacensem recepi, & corpus ejus surtim delatum Heloissa abbatissae & monialibus Paracleti concessi, authoritate omnipotentis Dei & omnium sanctorum, absolvo eum pro officio ab omnibus peccatis suis*
[20] *Studio tuo & mulieres omnes eviciti, & pene viros universos suparasti.* Abel Op.

from the originals, affirming we ought to follow the Greek version of the gospel of St. *Matthew* wrote in *Hebrew*. Without doubt, it was not a little surprising to St. Bernard, to hear a woman oppose him in a controversy, by citing a *Greek* text. 'Tis true, some authors say, *Abelard* made this answer to St. Bernard, after hearing from *Heloise* that objections were made to that form of prayer. However the case was, a woman with a small competency of learning might in those time pass for a miracle; and though she might not equal those descriptions which have been given of her, yet she may deservedly be placed in the rank of women of the greatest learning. Nor was she less remarkable for her piety, patience, and resignation, during her sicknesses in the latter part of her life. She died the 17th of May 1163. 'Tis said she desired to be buried in the same tomb with her *Abelard*, though that probably was not executed. Francis d'Amboise says, he saw at the convent the tombs of the founder and foundress near together. However a manuscript of Tours gives us an account of an extraordinary miracle which happened when *Abelard*'s grave was opened for *Heloise*'s body, namely that *Abelard* stretched out his arms to receive her, and embraced her closely, though there were twenty good years passed since he died. But that is a small matter to a writer of miracles.

I shall conclude this history with an epitaph on *Abelard*, which the Abbot of Clugni sent *Heloise*, and which is now to be read on his tomb; it hath nothing in it delicate either for thought or language, and will scarcely bear a translation. It is only added here for the sake of the curious, and as an instance of the respect paid to the memory of so great a man, and one whom envy had loaded with the greatest defamations.

"Petrus in hac petra latitat, quem mundus Homerum
  Clamabat, fed jam sidera sidus habent.
Sol erat hic Gallis, sed eum jam fata tulerunt:
  Ergo caret Regio Gallica sole suo.
Ille sciens quid quid fuit ulli scibile, vicit
  Artifices, artes absque docente docens.
Undecimae Maij petrum rapuere Calendae,
  Privantes Logices atria Rege fuo.
Est fatis, in tumulo Petrus hic jacit Abaelardus,
  Cui soli patuit scibile quid quid erat.

Gallorum Socrates, Plato maximus Hesperianum
Noster Aristoteles, Logicis (quicumque fuerunt)
Aut par aut melior; studioium cognitus orbi
Princeps, ingeuio varius, subtilius & acer,
Omnia vi superans rationis & arte loquendi,
Abaelardus erat. Sed nunc magis omnia vincit.
Cum Cluniacensem monacum, moremque professus,
Ad Christi veram transivit philosophiam,
In qua longaevae bene complens ultima vitae,
Philosophis quandoque bonis se connumerandum
Spem dedit, undenas Maio renovante Calendas."

Letter I. Abelard to Philintus.

It may be proper to acquaint the reader, that the following Letter was written by *Abelard* to a friend, to comfort him under some afflictions which had befallen him, by a recital of his own sufferings, which had been much heavier. It contains a particular account of his amour with *Heloise*, and the unhappy consequences of it. This Letter was written several years after *Abelard's* separation from *Heloise*.

The last time we were together, *Philintus*, you gave me a melancholy account of your misfortunes. I was sensibly touched with the relation, and, like a true friend, bore a share in your griefs. What did I not say to stop your tears? I laid before you all the reasons Philosophy could furnish, which I thought might any ways soften the strokes of Fortune: but all endeavours have proved useless: grief I perceive, has wholly seized your spirits: and your prudence, far from assisting, seems quite to have forsaken you. But my skilful friendship has found out an expedient to relieve you. Attend to me a moment; hear but the story of my misfortunes, and yours, *Philintus*, will be nothing, if you compare them with those of the loving and unhappy *Abelard*. Observe, I beseech you, at what expence I endeavour to serve you: and think this no small mark of my affection; for I am going to present you with the relation of such particulars, as it is impossible for me to recollect without piercing my heart with the most sensible affliction.

You know the place where I was born; but not perhaps that I was born with those complexional faults which strangers charge upon our nation, an extreme lightness of temper, and great inconstancy. I frankly own it, and shall be as free to acquaint you with those good qualities which were observed in me. I had a natural vivacity and aptness for all the polite arts. My father was a gentleman, and a man of good parts; he loved the wars, but differed in his sentiments from many who followed that profession. He thought it no praise to be illiterate, but in the camp he knew how to converse at the same time with the Muses and Bellona. He was the same in the management of his family, and took equal care to form his children to the study of polite learning as to their military exercises. As I was his eldest, and consequently his favourite son, he took more than ordinary care of my education. I had a natural genius to study, and made an extraordinary progress in it. Smitten with the love of books, and the praises which on all sides were bestowed upon me, I aspired to no reputation but what proceeded from learning. To my brothers I left the glory of battles, and the pomp of triumphs; nay more, I yielded them up my birthright and patrimony. I knew necessity was the great spur to study, and was afraid I should not merit the title of Learned, if I distinguished myself from others by nothing but a more plentiful fortune. Of all the sciences, Logic was the most to my taste. Such were the arms I chose to profess. Furnished with the weapons of reasoning, I took pleasure in going to public disputations to win trophies; and wherever I heard that this art flourished, I ranged like another Alexander, from province to province, to seek new adversaries, with whom I might try my strength.

The ambition I had to become formidable in logic led me at last to Paris, the centre of politeness, and where the science I was so smitten with had usually been in the greatest perfection. I put myself under the direction of one *Champeaux* a professor, who had acquired the character of the most skilful philosopher of his age, by negative excellencies only, by being the least ignorant. He received me with great demonstrations of kindness, but I was not so happy as to please him long: I was too knowing in the subjects he discoursed upon. I often confuted his notions: often in our disputations I pushed a good argument so home, that all his subtilty was not able to elude its force. It was impossible he should see himself surpassed by his scholar without resentment. It is sometimes dangerous to have too much merit.

Envy increased against me proportionably to my reputation. My enemies endeavoured to interrupt my progress, but their malice only provoked my courage; and measuring my abilities by the jealousy I had raised, I thought I had no farther occasion for Champeaux's lectures, but rather that I was sufficiently qualified to read to others. I stood for a place which was vacant at Melun. My master used all his artifice to defeat my hopes, but in vain; and on this occasion I triumphed over his cunning, as before I had done over his learning. My lectures were always crouded, and beginnings so fortunate, that I entirely obscured the renown of my famous master. Flushed with these happy conquests, I removed to Corbeil to attack the masters there, and so establish my character of the ablest Logician, the violence of travelling threw me into a dangerous distemper, and not being able to recover my strength, my physician, who perhaps were in a league with Champeaux, advised me to retire to my native air. Thus I voluntarily banished myself for some years. I leave you to imagine whether my absence was not regretted by the better sort. At length I recovered my health, when I received news that my greatest adversary had taken the habit of a monk. You may think was an act of penitence for having persecuted me; quite contrary, it was ambition; he resolved to raise himself to some church-dignity therefore he fell into the beaten track, and took on him the garb of feigned austerity; for this is the easiest and and shortest way to the highest ecclesiastical dignities. His wishes were successful, and he obtained a bishoprick: yet did he not quit Paris, and the care of the schools. He went to his diocese to gather in his revenues, but returned and passed the rest of his time in reading lectures to those few pupils which followed him. After this I often-engaged with him, and may reply to you as Ajax did to the Greeks;

"If you demand the fortune of that day,
When stak'd on this right hand your honours lay
If I did not oblige the foe to yield,
Yet did I never basely quit the field."

About this time my father Beranger, who to the age of sixty had lived very agreeably, retired from the world and shut himself up in a cloister, where he offered up to Heaven the languid remains of a life he could make no farther use of. My mother, who was yet young, took the same resolution. She turned a Religious, but did not entirely abandon the satisfactions of life. Her friends were continually at the grate; and the monastery, when one has an inclination to make it so, is exceeding charming and pleasant. I was present when my mother was professed. At my return I resolved to study divinity, and inquired for a director in that study. I was recommended to one *Anselm*, the very oracle of his time; but to give you my own opinion, one more venerable for his age and wrinkles than for his genius or learning. If you consulted him upon any difficulty, the sure consequence was to be much more uncertain in the point. Those who only saw him admired him, but those who reasoned with him were extremely dissatisfied. He was a great master of words, and talked much, but meant nothing. His discourse was a fire, which, instead of enlightening, obscured every thing with its smoke; a tree beautified with variety of leaves and branches, but barren. I came to him with a desire to learn, but found him like the fig-tree in the Gospel, or the old oak to which Lucan compares Pompey. I continued not long underneath his shadow. I took for my guides the primitive Fathers, and boldly launched into the ocean of the Holy Scriptures. In a short time I made such a progress, that others chose me for their director. The number of my scholars were incredible, and the gratuities I received from them were answerable to the great reputation I had acquired. Now I found myself safe in the harbour; the storms were passed, and the rage of my enemies had spent itself without effect. Happy, had I known to make a right use of this calm! But when the mind is most easy, it is most exposed to love, and even security here is the most dangerous state.

And now, my friend, I am going to expose to you all my weaknesses. All men, I believe, are under a necessity of paying tribute, at some time or other, to Love, and it is vain to strive to avoid it. I was a philosopher, yet this tyrant of the mind triumphed over all my wisdom; his darts were of greater force than all my reasoning, and with a sweet constraint he led me whither he pleased. Heaven, amidst an abundance of blessings with which I was intoxicated, threw in a heavy affliction. I became a most signal example of its vengeance; and the more unhappy, because having deprived me of the means of accomplishing my satisfaction, it left me to the fury of my criminal desires. I will tell you, my dear friend, the particulars of my story, and leave you to judge whether I deserved so severe a correction. I had always an aversion for those light women whom it is a reproach to pursue; I was ambitious in my choice, and wished to find some obstacles, that I might surmount them with the greater glory and pleasure.

There was in Paris a young creature, (ah! *Philintus!*) formed in a prodigality of Nature, to show mankind a finished composition; dear *Heloise!* the reputed niece of one *Fulbert* a canon. Her wit and her beauty would have fired the dullest and most insensible heart; and her education was equally admirable. *Heloise* was a mistress of the most polite arts. You may easily imagine that this did not a little help to captivate me. I saw her; I loved her; I resolved to endeavour to gain her affections. The thirst of glory cooled immediately in my heart, and all my passions were lost in this new one. I thought of nothing but *Heloise*; every thing brought her image to my mind. I was pensive, restless; and my passion was so violent as to admit of no restraint. I was always vain and presumptive; I flattered myself already with the most bewitching hopes. My reputation had spread itself every where; and could a virtuous lady resist a man that had confounded all the learned of the age? I was young;—could she show an infallibility to those vows which my heart never formed for any but herself? My person was advantageous enough and by my dress no one would have suspected me for a Doctor; and dress you know, is not a little engaging with women. Besides, I had wit enough to write a *billet doux*, and hoped, if ever she permitted my absent self to entertain her, she would read with pleasure those breathings of my heart.

Filled with these notions, I thought of nothing but the means to speak to her. Lovers either find or make all things easy. By the offices of common friends I gained the acquaintance of Fulbert. And, can you believe it, *Philintus*? he allowed me the privilege of his table, and an apartment in his house. I paid him, indeed, a considerable sum; for persons of his character do nothing without money. But what would I not have given! You my dear friend, know what love is; imagine then what a pleasure it must have been to a heart so inflamed as mine to be always so near the dear object of desire! I would not have exchanged my happy condition for that of the greatest monarch upon earth. I saw *Heloise*, I spoke to her: each action, each confused look, told her the trouble of my soul. And she, on the other side, gave me ground to hope for every thing from her generosity. Fulbert desired me to instruct her in philosophy; by this means I found opportunities of being in private with her and yet I was sure of all men the most timorous in declaring my passion.

As I was with her one day, alone, Charming *Heloise*, said I, blushing, if you know yourself, you will not be surprised with what passion you have inspired me with. Uncommon as it is, I can express it but with the common terms;—I love you, adorable *Heloise*! Till now I thought philosophy made us masters, of all our passions, and that it was a refuge from the storms in which weak mortals are tossed and shipwrecked; but you have destroyed my security, and broken this philosophic courage. I have despised riches; honour and its pageantries could never raise a weak thought in me; beauty alone hath fired my soul. Happy, if she who raised this passion kindly receives the declaration; but if it is an offence—No, replied *Heloise*; she must be very ignorant of your merit who can be offended at your passion. But, for my own repose, I wish either that you had not made this declaration, or that I were at liberty not to suspect your sincerity. Ah, divine *Heloise*, said I, flinging myself at her feet, I swear by yourself—I was going on to convince her of the truth of my passion, but heard a noise, and it was Fulbert. There was no avoiding it, but I must do a violence to my desire, and change the discourse to some other subject. After this I found frequent opportunities to free *Heloise* from those suspicions which the general insincerity of men had raised in her; and she too much desired what I said were truth, not to believe it. Thus there was a most happy understanding between us. The same house, the same love, united our persons and our desires. How many soft moments did we pass together! We took all opportunities to express to each other our mutual affections, and were ingenious in contriving incidents which might give us a plausible occasion for meeting. Pyramus and Thisbe's discovery of the crack in the wall was but a slight representation of our love and its sagacity. In the dead of night, when Fulbert and his domestics were in a sound sleep, we improved the time proper to the sweets of love. Not contenting ourselves, like those unfortunate loves, with giving insipid kisses to a wall, we made use of all the moments of our charming interviews. In the place where we met we had no lions to fear, and the study of philosophy served us for a blind. But I was so far from making any advances in the sciences that I lost all my taste of them; and when I was obliged to go from the sight of my dear mistress to my philosophical exercises, it was with the utmost regret and melancholy. Love is incapable of being concealed; a word, a look, nay silence, speaks it. My scholars discovered it first: they saw I had no longer that vivacity thought to which all things were easy: I could now do nothing but write verses to sooth my passion. I quitted Aristotle and his dry maxims, to practise the precepts of the more ingenious Ovid. No day passed in which I did not compose amorous verses. Love was my inspiring Apollo. My songs were spread abroad, and gained me frequent applauses. Those whom were in love as I was took a pride in learning them; and, by luckily applying my thoughts and verses, have obtained favours which, perhaps, they could not otherwise have gained. This gave our amours such an *eclat*, that the loves of *Heloise* and *Abelard* were the subject of all conversations.

The town-talk at last reached Fulbert's ears. It was with great difficulty he gave credit to what he heard, for he loved his niece, and was prejudiced in my favour; but, upon closer examination, he began to be less incredulous. He surprised us in one of our more soft conversations. How fatal, sometimes, are the consequences of curiosity! The anger of Fulbert seemed to moderate on this occasion, and I feared in the end some more heavy revenge. It is impossible to express the grief and regret which filled my soul when I was obliged to leave the canon's house and my dear *Heloise*. But this separation of our persons the more firmly united our minds; and the desperate condition we were reduced to, made us capable of attempting any thing.

My intrigues gave me but little shame, so lovingly did I esteem the occasion. Think what the gay young divinities said, when Vulcan caught Mars and the goddess of Beauty in his net, and impute it all to me. Fulbert surprised me with *Heloise*, and what man that had a soul in him would not have borne any ignominy on the same conditions? The next day I provided myself of a private lodging near the loved house, being resolved not to abandon my prey. I continued some time without appearing publickly. Ah, how long did those few moments seem to me! When we fall from a state of happiness, with what impatience do we bear our misfortunes!

It being impossible that I could live without seeing *Heloise*, I endeavoured to engage her servant, whose name was *Agaton*, in my interest. She was brown, well shaped, a person superior to the ordinary rank; her features regular, and her eyes sparkling; fit to raise love in any man whose heart was not prepossessed by another passion. I met her alone, and intreated her to have pity on a distressed lover. She answered, she would undertake any thing to serve me, but there was a reward.—At these words I opened my purse and showed the shining metal, which lays asleep guards, forces away through rocks, and softens the hearts of the most obdurate fair. You are mistaken, said she, smiling, and shaking her head—you do not know me. Could gold tempt me, a rich abbot takes his nightly station, and sings under my window: he offers to send me to his abbey, which, he says, is situate in the most pleasant country in the world. A courtier offers me a considerable sum of money, and assures me I need have no apprehensions; for if our amours have consequences, he will marry me to his gentleman, and give him a handsome employment. To say nothing of a young officer, who patroles about here every night, and makes his attacks after all imaginable forms. It must be Love only which could oblige him to follow me; for I have not like your great ladies, any rings or jewels to tempt him: yet, during all his siege of love, his feather and his embroidered coat have not made any breach in my heart. I shall not quickly be brought to capitulate, I am too faithful to my first conqueror—and then she looked earnestly on me. I answered, I did not understand her discourse. She replied, For a man of sense and gallantry you have a very slow apprehension; I am in love with you *Abelard*. I know you adore *Heloise*, I do not blame you; I desire only to enjoy the second place in your affections. I have a tender heart as well as my mistress; you may without difficulty make returns to my passion. Do not perplex yourself with unfashionable scruples; a prudent man ought to love several at the same time; if one should fail, he is not then left unprovided.

You cannot imagine, *Philintus*, how much I was surprised at these words. So entirely did I love *Heloise* that without reflecting whether Agaton spoke any thing reasonable or not, I immediately left her. When I had gone a little way from her I looked back, and saw her biting her nails in the rage of disappointment, which made me fear some fatal consequences. She hastened to Fulbert, and told him the offer I had made her, but I suppose concealed the other part of the story. The Canon never forgave this affront. I afterwards perceived he was more deeply concerned for his niece than I at first imagined. Let no lover hereafter follow my example, A woman rejected is an outrageous creature. Agaton was day and night at her window on purpose to keep me at a distance from her mistress, and so gave her own gallants opportunity enough to display their several abilities.

I was infinitely perplexed what course to take; at last I applied to *Heloise* singing-master. The shining metal, which had no effect on Agaton, charmed him; he was excellently qualified for conveying a billet with the greatest dexterity and secrecy. He delivered one of mine to *Heloise*, who, according to my appointment was ready at the end of a garden, the wall of which I scaled by a ladder of ropes. I confess to you all my failings, *Philintus*. How would my enemies, Champeaux and Anselm, have triumphed, had they seen the redoubted philosopher in such a wretched condition? Well—I met my soul's joy, my *Heloise*. I shall not describe our transports, they were not long; for the first news *Heloise* acquainted me with plunged me in a thousand distractions. A floating *delos* was to be sought for, where she might be safely delivered of a burthen she began already to feel.

Without losing much time in debating, I made her presently quit the Canon's house, and at break of day depart for Britany; where, she like another goddess, gave the world another Apollo, which my sister took care of.

This carrying off *Heloise* was sufficient revenge upon Fulbert. It filled him with the deepest concern, and had like to have deprived him of all the little share of wit which Heaven had allowed him. His sorrow and lamentation gave the censorious an occasion of suspecting him for something more than the uncle of *Heloise*.

In short, I began to pity his misfortune, and think this robbery which love had made me commit was a sort of treason. I endeavoured to appease his anger by a sincere confession of all that was past, and by hearty engagements to marry *Heloise* secretly. He gave me his consent and with many protestations and embraces confirmed our reconciliation. But what dependence can be made on the word of an ignorant devotee. He was only plotting a cruel revenge, as you will see by what follows.

I took a journey into Britany, in order to bring back my dear *Heloise*, whom I now considered as my wife. When I had acquainted her with what had passed between the Canon and me, I found she was of a contrary opinion to me. She urged all that was possible to divert me from marriage: that it was a bond always fatal to a philosopher; that the cries of children, and cares of a family, were utterly inconsistent with the tranquility and application which the study of philosophy required. She quoted to me all that was written on the subject by Theophrastus, Cicero, and, above all, insisted on the unfortunate Socrates, who quitted life with joy, because by that means he left Xantippe. Will it not be more agreeable to me, said she, to see myself your mistress than your wife? and will not love have more power than marriage to keep our hearts firmly united? Pleasures tasted sparingly, and with difficulty, have always a higher relish, while every thing, by being easy and common, grows flat and insipid.

I was unmoved by all this reasoning. *Heloise* prevailed upon my sister to engage me. Lucille (for that was her name) taking me aside one day, said, What do you intend, brother? Is it possible that *Abelard* should in earnest think of marrying *Heloise*? She seems indeed to deserve a perpetual affection; beauty, youth, and learning, all that can make a person valuble, meet in her. You may adore all this if you please; but not to flatter you, what is beauty but a flower, which may be blasted by the least fit of sickness? When those features, with which you have been so captivated, shall be sunk, and those graces lost, you will too late repent that you have entangled yourself in a chain, from which death only can free you. I shall see you reduced to the married man's only hope of survivorship. Do you think learning ought to make *Heloise* more amiable? I know she is not one of those affected females who are continually oppressing you with fine speeches, criticising books, and deciding upon the merit of authors, When such a one is in the fury of her discourse, husbands, friends, servants, all fly before her. *Heloise* has not this fault; yet it is troublesome not to be at liberty to use the least improper expression before a wife, that you bear with pleasure from a mistress.

But you say, you are sure of the affections of *Heloise* I believe it; she has given you no ordinary proofs. But can you be sure marriage will not be the tomb of her love? The name of Husband and Master are always harsh, and *Heloise* will not be the phenix you now think her. Will she not be a woman? Come, come, the head of a philosopher is less secure than those of other men. My sister grew warm in the argument, and was going to give me a hundred more reasons of this kind; but I angrily interrupted her, telling her only, that she did not know *Heloise*.

A few days after, we departed together from Britany, and came to Paris, where I completed my project. It was my intent my marriage should be kept secret, and therefore *Heloise* retired among the nuns of Argenteuil.

I now thought Fulbert's anger disarmed; I lived in peace: but, alas! our marriage proved but a weak defence against his revenge. Observe, *Philintus*, to what a barbarity he pursued it! He bribed my servants; an assassin came into my bed chamber by night with a razor in his hand, and found me in a deep sleep. I suffered the most shameful punishment that the revenge of an enemy could invent; in short without losing my life, I lost my manhood. I was punished indeed in the offending part; the desire was left me, but not the possibility of satisfying the passion. So cruel an action escaped not unpunished; the villain suffered the same infliction; poor comfort for so irretrievable an evil; I confess to you, shame, more than any sincere penitence; made me resolve to hide myself from my *Heloise*. Jealousy took possession of my mind; at the very expence of her happiness I decreed to disappoint all rivals. Before I put myself in a cloister, I obliged her to take the habit, and retire into the nunnery of Argenteuil. I remember somebody would have opposed her making such a cruel sacrifice of herself, but she answered in the words of Cornelia, after the death of Pompey the Great;

> *"—O conjux, ego te scelereta peremi,*
> *—Te fata extrema petente*
> *Vita digna fui? Moriar——&c.*
>
> *O my lov'd lord! our fatal marriage draws*
> *On thee this doom, and I the guilty cause!*
> *Then whilst thou go'st th' extremes of Fate to prove,*
> *I'll share that fate, and expiate thus my love."*

Speaking these verses, she marched up to the altar, and took the veil with a constancy which I could not have expected in a woman who had so high a taste of pleasure which she might still enjoy. I blushed at my own weakness; and without deliberating a moment longer, I buried myself in a cloister, resolving to vanquish a fruitless passion. I now reflected that God had chastised me thus grievously, that he might save me from that destruction in which I had like to have been swallowed up. In order to avoid idleness, the unhappy incendiary of those criminal flames which had ruined me in the world, I endeavoured in my retirement to put those talents to a good use which I had before so much abused. I gave the novices rules of divinity agreeable to the holy fathers and councils. In the mean while, the enemies which my fame had raised up, and especially Alberic and Lotulf, who after the death of their masters Champeaux and Anselm affirmed the sovereignty of learning, began to attack me. They loaded me with the falsest imputations, and, notwithstanding all my defence, I had the mortification to see my books condemned by a council and burnt. This was a cutting sorrow, and, believe me, *Philintus*, the former calamity suffered by the cruelty of Fulbert was nothing in comparison to this.

The affront I had newly received, and the scandalous debaucheries of the monks, obliged me to banish myself, and retire near Nogent. I lived in a desart, where I flattered myself I should avoid fame, and be secure from the malice of my enemies. I was again deceived. The desire of being taught by me, drew crowds of auditors even thither. Many left the towns and their houses, and came and lived in tents; for herbs, coarse fare, and hard lodging, they abandoned the delicacies of a plentiful table and easy life. I looked like a prophet in the wilderness attended by his disciples. My lectures were perfectly clear from all that had been condemned. And happy had it been if our solitude had been inaccessible to Envy! With the considerable gratuities I received I built a chapel, and dedicated it to the Holy Ghost, by the name of the Paraclete. The rage of my enemies now awakened again, and forced me to quit this retreat. This I did without much difficulty. But first the Bishop of Troies gave me leave to establish there a nunnery, which I did, and committed the care of it to my dear *Heloise*. When I had settled her here, can you believe it, *Philintus*? I left her without taking any leave. I did not wander long without settled habitation; for the Duke of Britany, informed of my misfortunes, named me to the Abbey of *Guildas*, where I now am, and where I now suffer every day fresh persecutions.

I live in a barbarous country, the language of which I do not understand. I have no conversation with the rudest people. My walks are on the inaccessible shore of a sea which is perpetually stormy. My monks are known by their dissoluteness, and living without rule or order. Could you see the abbey *Philintus*, you would not call it one. The doors and walls are without any ornament except the heads of wild boars and hinds' feet, which are nailed up against them, and the heads of frightful animals. The cells are hung with the skins of deer. The monks have not so much as a bell to wake them; the cocks and dogs supply that defect. In short, they pass their whole days in hunting; would to Heaven that were their greatest fault, or that their pleasures terminated there! I endeavour in vain to recall them to their duty; they all combine against me, and I only expose myself to continual vexations and dangers. I imagine that every moment a naked sword hang over my head. Sometimes they surround me and load me with infinite abuses; sometimes they abandon me, and I am left alone to my own tormenting thoughts. I make it my endeavour to merit by my sufferings, and to appease an angry God. Sometimes I grieve for the house of the *Paraclete*, and wish to see it again. Ah, *Philintus*! does not the love of *Heloise* still burn in my heart? I have not yet triumphed over that happy passion. In the midst of my retirement I sigh, I weep, I pine, I speak the dear name of *Heloise*, pleased to hear the sound, I complain of the severity of Heaven. But, oh! let us not deceive ourselves: I have not made a right use of grace. I am thoroughly wretched. I have not yet torn from my heart deep roots which vice has planted in it. For if my conversion was sincere, how could I take a pleasure to relate my past follies? Could I not more easily comfort myself in my afflictions? Could I not turn to my advantage those words of God himself, *If they have persecuted me, they will also persecute you; if the world hate you, ye know that it hated me also*? Come *Philintus*, let us make a strong effort, turn our misfortunes to our advantage, make them meritorious, or at least wipe out our offences; let us receive, without murmuring, what comes from the hand of God, and let us not oppose our will to his. Adieu. I give you advice, which could I myself follow, I should be happy.

Letter II. Heloise to Abelard.

The foregoing Letter would probably not have produced any others, if it had been delivered to the person to whom it was directed; but falling by accident into *Heloise's* hands, who knew the character she opened it and read it; and by that means her former passion being awakened, she immediately set herself to write to her husband as follows.

Domino suo, imo Patri; Conjugi suo, imo Fratri; Ancilla sua, imo Filia; ipsius Uxor, imo Soror; Abaelardo Heloisa, &c. Abel. Op.[21]

A consolatory letter of yours to a friend happened some days since to fall into my hands. My knowledge of the character, and my love of the hand, soon gave me the curiosity to open it. In justification of the liberty I took, I flattered myself I might claim a sovereign privilege over every thing which came from you nor was I scrupulous to break thro' the rules of good breeding, when it was to hear news of *Abelard.* But how much did my curiosity cost me? what disturbance did it occasion? and how was I surprised to find the whole letter filled with a particular and melancholy account of our misfortunes? I met with my name a hundred times; I never saw it without fear: some heavy calamity always, followed it, I saw yours too, equally unhappy. These mournful but dear remembrances, puts my spirits into such a violent motion, that I thought it was too much to offer comfort to a friend for a few slight disgraces by such extraordinary means, as the representation of our sufferings and revolutions. What reflections did I not make, I began to consider the whole afresh, and perceived myself pressed with the same weight of grief as when we first began to be miserable. Tho' length of time ought to have closed up my wounds, yet the seeing them described by your hand was sufficient to make them all open and bleed afresh. Nothing can ever blot from my memory what you have suffered in defence of your writings. I cannot help thinking of the rancorous malice of Alberic and Lotulf. A cruel uncle and an injured lover, will be always present to my aking sight. I shall never forget what enemies your learning, and what envy your

---

[21] To her Lord, her Father; her Husband, her Brother; his Servant his Child; his Wife, his Sister; and to express all that is humble, respectful and loving to her *Abelard, Heloise* writes this.

glory, raised against you. I shall never forget your reputation, so justly acquired, torn to pieces, and blasted by the inexorable cruelty of half-learned pretenders to science. Was not your Treatise of Divinity condemned to be burnt? Were you not threatened with perpetual imprisonment? In vain you urged in your defence, that your enemies imposed on you opinions quite different from your meaning; in vain you condemned those opinions; all was of no effect towards your justification; it was resolved you should be a heretic. What did not those two false prophets[22] accuse you of, who declaimed so severely against you before the Council of Sens? What scandals were vented on occasion of the name Paraclete given to your chapel? What a storm was raised against you by the treacherous monks, when you did them the honour to be called their Brother? This history of our numerous misfortunes, related in so true and moving a manner, made my heart bleed within me. My tears, which I could not restrain, have blotted half your letter: I wish they had effaced the whole and that I had returned it to you in that condition. I should then have been satisfied with the little time; kept it, but it was demanded of me too soon.

I must confess I was much easier in my mind before I read your letter. Sure all the misfortunes of lovers are conveyed to them thro' their eyes. Upon reading your letter I felt all mine renewed, I reproached myself for having been so long without venting my sorrows, when the rage of our unrelenting enemies still burns with the same fury. Since length of time, which disarms the strongest hatred, seems but to aggravate theirs; since it is decreed that your virtue shall be persecuted till it takes refuge in the grave, and even beyond that, your ashes perhaps, will not be suffered to rest in peace,—let me always meditate on your calamities, let me publish them thro' all the world, if possible, to shame an age that has not known how to value you. I will spare no one, since no one would interest himself to protect you, and your enemies are never weary of oppressing your innocence, Alas! my memory is perpetually filled with bitter remembrances of past evils, and are there more to be feared still? shall my *Abelard* be never mentioned without tears? shall thy dear name be never spoken but with sighs? Observe, I beseech you, to what a wretched condition you have reduced me: sad, afflicted, without any possible comfort, unless it proceed from you. Be not then

---

[22] St. Bernard and St. Norbet.

unkind, nor deny, I beg you that little relief which you can only give. Let me have a faithful account of all that concerns you. I would know every thing, be it ever so unfortunate. Perhaps, by mingling my sighs with yours, I may make your sufferings less, if that observation be true, that all sorrows divided are made lighter.

Tell me not, by way of excuse, you will spare our tears; the tears of women, shut up in a melancholy place, and devoted to penitence, are not to be spared. And if you wait for an opportunity to write pleasant and agreeable things to us, you will delay writing too long. Prosperity seldom chuses the side of the virtuous; and Fortune is so blind, that in a crowd in which there is perhaps but one wife and brave man, it is not to be expected she should single him out. Write to me then immediately, and wait not for miracles; they are too scarce, and we too much accustomed to misfortunes to expect any happy turn. I shall always have this, if you please, and this will be always agreeable to me, that when I receive any letters from you, I shall know you still remember me. Seneca, (with whose writings you made me acquainted,) as much a Stoic as he was, seemed to be so very sensible of this kind of pleasure, that upon opening any letters from Lucilius, he imagined he felt the same delight as when they conversed together.

I have made it an observation, since our absence, that we are much fonder of the pictures of those we love, when they are at a great distance, than when they are near to us. It seems to me, as if the farther they are removed their pictures grow the more finished, and acquire a greater resemblance; at least, our imagination, which perpetually figures them to us by the desire we have of seeing them again, makes us think so. By a peculiar power, Love can make that seem life itself, which, as soon as the loved object returns, is nothing but a little canvas and dead colours. I have your picture in my room; I never pass by it without stopping to look at it; and yet when you were present with me, I scarce ever cast my eyes upon it. If a picture, which is but a mute representation of an object, can give such pleasure, what cannot letters inspire? They have souls; they can speak; they have in them all that force which expresses the transports of the heart; they have all the fire of our passions; they can raise them as much as if the persons themselves were present; they have all the softness and delicacy of speech, and sometimes a boldness of expression even beyond it.

~ 51 ~

Pierre Abelard

We may write to each other; so innocent a pleasure is not forbidden us. Let us not lose, through negligence, the only happiness which is left us, and the only one, perhaps, which the malice of our enemies can never ravish from us. I shall read that you are my husband, and you shall see me address you as a wife. In spite of all your misfortunes, you may be what you please in your letter. Letters were first invented for comforting such solitary wretches as myself. Having lost the substantial pleasures of seeing and possessing you, I shall in some measure compensate this loss by the satisfaction I shall find in your writing. There I shall read your most secret thoughts; I shall carry them always about me; I shall kiss them every moment: if you can be capable of any jealousy, let it be for the fond caresses I shall bestow on your letters, and envy only the happiness of those rivals. That writing may be no trouble to you, write always to me carelessly, and without study: I had rather read the dictates of the heart than of the brain. I cannot live if you do not tell me you always love me; but that language ought to be so natural to you, that I believe you cannot speak otherwise to me without great violence to yourself. And since, by that melancholy relation to your friend, you have awakened all my sorrows, it is but reasonable you should allay them by some marks of an inviolable love.

I do not, however, reproach you for the innocent artifice you made use of to comfort a person in affliction, by comparing his misfortune to another much greater. Charity is ingenious in finding out such pious artifices, and to be commended for using them. But do you owe nothing more to us than to that friend, be the friendship between you ever so intimate? We are called your sisters; we call ourselves your Children; and if it were possible to think of any expression which could signify a dearer relation, or a more affectionate regard and mutual obligation between us, we would use them: if we could be so ungrateful as not to speak our just acknowledgments to you, this church, these altars, these Walls, would reproach our silence, and speak for us, But without leaving it to that, it will be always a pleasure to me to say, that you only are the founder of this house; it is wholly your work. You, by inhabiting here, have given fame and function to a place known before only for robberies and murders. You have, in the literal sense, made the den of thieves a house of prayer. These cloisters owe nothing to public charities; our walls were not raised by the usury of publicans, nor their foundations laid in base extortion. The God whom we serve sees nothing but innocent riches and harmless votaries, whom you have placed here.

Whatever this young vineyard is, is owing all to you; and it is your part to employ your whole care to cultivate and improve it; this ought to be one of the principal affairs of your life. Though our holy renunciation, our vows, and our manner of life, seem to secure us from all temptations; though our walls and grates prohibit all approaches, yet it is the outside only, the bark of the tree is covered from injuries; while the sap of original corruption may imperceptibly spread within, even to the heart, and prove fatal to the most promising plantation, unless continual care be taken to cultivate and secure it. Virtue in us is grafted upon Nature and the Woman; the one is weak, and the other is always changeable. To plant the Lord's vine is a work of no little labour; and after it is planted it will require great application and diligence to manure it. The Apostle of the Gentiles; as great a labourer as he was, says, *He hath planted, and Apollo hath watered; but it is God that giveth the increase.* Paul had planted the Gospel among the Corinthians, by his holy and earnest preaching; *Apollos*, a zealous disciple of that great master, continued to cultivate it by frequent exhortations; and the grace of God, which their constant prayers, implored for that church, made the endeavours of both successful.

This ought to be an example for your conduct towards us. I know you are not slothful; yet your labours are not directed to us; your cares are wasted upon a set of men whose thoughts are only earthly, and you refuse to reach out your hand to support those who are weak and staggering in their way to heaven, and who, with all their endeavours, can scarcely preserve themselves from falling. You fling the pearls of the gospel before swine, when you speak to those who are filled with the good things of this world, and nourished with the fatness of the earth; and you neglect the innocent sheep, who, tender as they are, would yet follow you thro' deserts and mountains. Why are such pains thrown away upon the ungrateful, while not a thought is bestowed upon your children, whose souls would be filled with a sense of your goodness? But why should I intreat you in the name of your children? Is it possible I should fear obtaining any thing of you, when I ask it in my own name? And must I use any other prayers than my own to prevail upon you? The St. Austins, Tertullians, and Jeromes, have wrote to the Eudoxas, Paulas, and Melanias; and can you read those names, though of saints, and not remember mine? Can it be criminal for you to imitate St. Jerome, and discourse with me concerning the Scripture? or Tertullian, and preach mortification? or St. Austin, and explain to me the nature of grace? Why should I only reap no advantage from your learning? When you write to me, you will write to your wife. Marriage has made such a correspondence lawful; and since you can, without giving the least scandal, satisfy me, why will you not? I have a barbarous uncle, whose inhumanity is a security against any criminal desire which tenderness and the remembrance of our past enjoyments might inspire. There is nothing that can cause you any fear; you need not fly to conquer. You may see me, hear my sighs, and be a witness of all my sorrows, without incurring any danger, since you can only relieve me with tears and words. If I have put myself into a cloister with reason, persuade me to continue in it with devotion: you have been the occasion of all my misfortunes, you therefore must be the instrument of all my comforts.

You cannot but remember, (for what do not lovers remember?) with what pleasure I have past whole days in hearing your discourse. How, when you were absent, I shut myself from everyone to write to you; how uneasy I was till my letter had come to your hands; what artful management it required to engage confidents. This detail, perhaps, surprises you, and you are in pain for what will fellow. But I am no longer ashamed that my passion has had no bounds for you; for I have done more than all this: I have hated myself that I might love you; I came hither to ruin myself in a perpetual imprisonment, that I might make you live quiet and easy. Nothing but virtue, joined to a love perfectly disengaged from the commerce of the senses, could have produced such effect. Vice never inspires any thing like this; it is too much enslaved to the body. When we love pleasures, we love the living, and not the dead; we leave off burning with desire for those who can no longer burn for us. This was my cruel uncle's notions; he measured my virtue by the frailty of my sex, and thought it was the man, and not the person, I loved. But he has been guilty to no purpose. I love you more than ever; and to revenge myself of him, I will still love you with all the tenderness of my soul till the last moment of my life. If formerly my affection for you was not so pure, if in those days the mind and the body shared in the pleasure of loving you, I often told you, even then, that I was more pleased with possessing your heart than with any other happiness, and the man was the thing I least valued in you.

You cannot but be entirely persuaded of this by the extreme unwillingness I showed to marry you: tho' I knew that the name of Wife was honourable in the world, and holy in religion, yet the name of your mistress had greater charms, because it was more free. The bonds of matrimony, however honourable, still bear with them a necessary engagement; and I was very unwilling to be necessitated to love always a man who, perhaps, would not always love me. I despised the name of Wife, that I might live happy with that of Mistress; and I find, by your letter to your friend, you have not forgot that delicacy of passion in a woman who loved you always with the utmost tenderness, and yet wished to love you more, you have very justly observed in your letter, that I esteemed those public engagements insipid which form alliances only to be dissolved by death, and which put life and love under the same unhappy necessity. But you have not added how often I have made protestations that it was infinitely preferable to me to live with *Abelard* as his mistress than with any other as empress of the world, and that I was more happy in obeying you, than I should have been in lawfully captivating the lord of the universe. Riches and pomp are not the charms of love. True tenderness make us to separate the lover from all that is external to him, and setting aside his quality, fortune, and employments, consider him singly by himself.

'Tis not love, but the desire of riches and honour, which makes women run into the embraces of an indolent husband. Ambition, not affection, forms such marriages. I believe indeed they may be followed with some honours and advantages, but I can never think that this is the way to enjoy the pleasures of an affectionate union, nor to feel those secret and charming emotions of hearts that have long strove to be united. These martyrs of marriage pine always for large fortunes, which they think they have lost. The wife sees husbands richer that her own, and the husband wives better portioned than his. Their interested vows occasion regret, and regret produces hatred. They soon part, or always desire it. This restless and tormenting passion punishes them for aiming at other advantages of love than love itself.

If there is any thing which may properly be called happiness here below, I am persuaded it is in the union of two persons who love each other with perfect liberty, who are united by a secret inclination, and satisfied with each other's merit; their hearts are full and leave no vacancy for any other passion; they enjoy perpetual tranquillity, because they enjoy content.

Pierre Abelard

If I could believe you as truly persuaded of my merit as I am of yours, I might say there has been such a time when we were such a pair. Alas! how was it possible I should not be certain of your merit? If I could ever have doubted it, the universal esteem would have made me determine in your favour. What country, what city, has not desired your presence? Could you ever retire but you drew the eyes and hearts of all after you? Did not every one rejoice in having seen you? Even women, breaking through the laws of decorum, which custom had imposed upon them, showed manifestly they felt something more for you than esteem. I have known some who have been profuse in their husband's praises, who have yet envied my happiness, and given strong intimations they could have refused you nothing. But what could resist you? Your reputation, which so much soothed the vanity of our sex; your air, your manner; that life in your eyes, which so admirably expressed the vivacity of your mind; your conversation with that ease and elegance which gave every thing you spoke such an agreeable and insinuating turn; in short, every thing spoke for you; very different from some mere scholars, who, with all their learning, have not the capacity to keep up an ordinary conversation, and with all their wit cannot win the affection of women who have a much less share than themselves.

With what ease did you compose verses? and yet those ingenious trifles, which were but a recreation after your more serious studies, are still the entertainment and delight of persons of the best taste. The smallest song, nay, the least sketch of any thing you made for me, had a thousand beauties capable of making it last as long as there are love or lovers in the world. Thus those songs will be sung in honour of other women which you designed only for me? and those tender and natural expressions which spoke your love will help others to explain their passion, with much more advantage than what they themselves are capable of.

What rivals did your gallantries of this kind occasion me? How many ladies laid claim to them? 'Twas a tribute their self-love paid to their beauty. How many have I seen with sighs declare their passion for you, when, after some common visit you had made them, they chanced to be complimented for the Sylvia of your poems? others, in despair and envy, have reproached me, that I had no charms but what your wit bestowed on me, nor in any thing the advantage over them but in being beloved by you. Can you believe if I tell you, that, notwithstanding the vanity of my sex, I thought myself peculiarly happy in having a lover to whom I was obliged for my charms, and took a secret pleasure in being admired by a man who, when he pleased, could raise his mistress to the character of a goddess? Pleased with your glory only, I read with delight all those praises you offered me, and without reflecting how little I deserved, I believed myself such as you described me, that I might be more certain I pleased you.

But oh! where is that happy time fled? I now lament my lover, and of all my joys there remains nothing but the painful remembrance that *they are past.* Now learn, all you my rivals who once viewed my happiness with such jealous eyes, that he you once envied me can never more be yours or mine. I loved him, my love was his crime, and the cause of his punishment. My beauty once charmed him: pleased with each other, we passed our brightest days in tranquillity and happiness. If that was a crime, 'tis a crime I am yet fond of, and I have no other regret, than that against my will I must necessarily be innocent. But what do I say? My misfortune was to have cruel relations, whose malice disturbed the calm we enjoyed. Had they been capable of the returns of reason, I had now been happy in the enjoyment of my dear husband. Oh! how cruel were they when their blind fury urged a villain to surprise you in your sleep! Where was I? Where was your *Heloise* then? What joy should I have had in defending my lover! I would have guarded you from violence, though at the expence of my life; my cries and the shrieks alone would have stopped the hand.—! Oh! whither does the excess of passion hurry me? Here love is shocked, and modesty, joined with despair, deprive me of words. 'Tis eloquence to be silent, where no expression can reach the greatness of the misfortune.

But, tell me, whence proceeds your neglect of me since my being professed? You know nothing moved me to it but your disgrace, nor did I give any consent but yours. Let me hear what is the occasion of your coldness, or give me leave to tell you now my opinion. Was it not the sole view of pleasure which engaged you to me? and has not my tenderness, by leaving you nothing to wish for, extinguished your desires? Wretched *Heloise!* You could please when you wished to avoid it; you merited incense, when you could remove to a distance the hand that offered it; but since your heart has been softened, and has yielded; since you have devoted and sacrificed yourself, you are deserted and forgotten. I am convinced, by sad experience, that it is natural to avoid those to whom we have been too much obliged; and that uncommon generosity produces neglect rather than acknowledgement. My heart surrendered too soon to gain the esteem of the conqueror; you took it without difficulty, and give it up easily. But, ungrateful as you are, I will never content to it. And though in this place I ought not to retain a wish of my own, yet I have ever secretly preserved the desire of being beloved by you. When I pronounced my sad vow, I then had about me your last letter, in which you protested you would be wholly mine, and would never live but to love me. 'Tis to you, therefore, I have offered myself; you had my heart, and I had yours; do not demand any thing back; you must bear with my passion as a thing which of right belongs to you, and from which you can no ways be disengaged.

Alas! what folly is it to talk at this rate? I see nothing here but marks of the Deity, and I speak of nothing but man! You have been the cruel occasion of this by your conduct. Unfaithful man! ought you at once to break off loving me. Why did you not deceive me for a while, rather than immediately abandon me? If you had given me at least but some faint signs even of a dying passion, I myself had favoured the deception. But in vain would I flatter myself that you could be constant; you have left me no colour of making your excuse. I am earnestly desirous to see you; but if that be impossible, I will content myself with a few lines from your hand. Is it so hard for one who loves to write? I ask for none of your letters filled with learning, and writ for reputation; all I desire is such letters as the heart dictates, and which the hand can scarce write fast enough. How did I deceive myself with the hopes that you would be wholly mine when I took the veil, and engaged myself to live for ever under your laws? For in being professed, I vowed no more than to be yours only, and I obliged myself voluntarily to a confinement in which you desired to place me. Death only then can make me leave the place where you have fixed me; and then too, my ashes shall rest, here and wait for your, in order to shew my obedience and devotedness to you to the latest moment possible.

Why should I conceal from you the secret of my call? You know it was neither zeal nor devotion which led me to the cloister. Your conscience is too faithful a witness to permit you to disown it. Yet here I am, and here I will remain; to this place an unfortunate love, and my cruel relations, have condemned me. But if you do not continue your concern for me, If I lose your affection, what have I gained by my imprisonment? What recompense can I hope for? The unhappy consequence of a criminal conduit, and your disgraces, have put on me this habit of chastity, and not the sincere desire of being truly penitent. Thus I strive and labour in vain. Among those whose are wedded to God I serve a man: among the heroic supporters of the Cross, I am a poor slave to a human passion: at the head of a religious community I am devoted to *Abelard* only. What a prodigy am I? Enlighten me, O Lord! Does thy grace or my own despair draw these words from me? I am sensible I am in the Temple of Chastity, covered only with the ashes of that fire which hath consumed us. I am here, I confess, a sinner, but one who, far from weeping for her sins, weeps only for her lover; far from abhorring her crimes, endeavours only to add to them; and who, with a weakness unbecoming the state I am in, please myself continually with the remembrance of past actions, when it is impossible to renew them.

Good God! what is all this! I reproach myself for my own faults, I accuse you for yours, and to what purpose? Veiled as I am, behold in what a disorder you have plunged me! How difficult is it to fight always for duty against inclination? I know what obligations this veil lays on me, but I feel more strongly what power a long habitual passion has over my heart. I am conquered by my inclination. My love troubles my mind, and disorders my will. Sometimes I am swayed by the sentiments of piety which arise in me, and the next moment I yield up my imagination to all that is amorous and tender. I tell you to-day what I would not have said to you yesterday. I had resolved to love you no more; I considered I had made a vow, taken the veil, and am as it were dead and buried; yet there rises unexpectedly from the bottom of my heart a passion which triumphs over all these notions, and darkens all my reason and devotion. You reign in such inward retreats of my soul, that I know not where to attack you. When I endeavour to break those chains by which I am bound to you, I only deceive myself, and all the efforts I am able to make serve but to bind them the faster. Oh, for Pity's sake help a wretch to renounce her desires herself, and if it be possible, even to renounce you! If you are a lover, a father, help a mistress, comfort a child! These tender names, cannot they move you? Yield either to pity or love. If you gratify my request I shall continue a Religious without longer profaning my calling. I am ready to humble myself with you to the wonderful providence of God, who does all things for our sanctification; who, by his grace, pacifies all that is vicious and corrupt in the principle, and; by the inconceivable riches of his mercy, draws us to himself against our wishes, and by degrees opens our eyes to discern the greatness of his bounty, which at first we would not understand.

I thought to end my letter here. But now I am complaining against you, I must unload my heart, and tell you all its jealousies, and reproaches. Indeed I thought it something hard, that when we had both engaged to consecrate ourselves to Heaven, you should insist upon doing it first. Does *Abelard* then, said I, suspect he shall see renewed in me the example of Lot's wife, who could not forbear looking back when she left Sodom? If my youth and sex might give occasion of fear that I should return to the world, could not my behaviour, my fidelity, and this heart which you ought to know, could not banish such ungenerous apprehensions? This distrustful foresight touched me sensibly. I said to myself, there was a time when he could rely upon my bare word, and does he now want vows to secure himself of me? What occasion have I given him in the whole course of my life to admit the least suspicion? I could meet him at all his assignations, and would I decline following him to the feats of holiness? I who have not refused to be a victim of pleasure to gratify him, can he think I would refuse to be a sacrifice of honour to obey him? Has Vice such charms to well-born souls? and, when we have once drank of the cup of sinners, is it with such difficulty that we take the chalice of saints? Or did you believe yourself a greater master to teach vice than virtue, or did you think it was more easy to persuade me to the first than the latter? No, this suspicion would be injurious to both. Virtue is too amiable not to be embraced, when you reveal her charms; and Vice too hideous not to be avoided, when you show her deformities. Nay, when you please, any thing seems lovely to me, and nothing is frightful or difficult when you are by. I am only weak when I am alone and unsupported by you, and therefore it depends on you alone that I may be such as you desire. I wish to Heav'n you had not such a power over me. If you had any occasion to fear, you would be less negligent. But what is there for you to fear? I have done too much, and now have nothing more to do but to triumph over your ingratitude. When we lived happy together, you might have made it doubt whether pleasure or affection united me more to you; but the place from whence I write to you must now have entirely taken away that doubt. Even here I love you as much as ever I did in the world. If I had loved pleasures, could I not yet have found means to have gratified myself? I was not above twenty-two years old; and there were other men left though I was deprived of *Abelard* and yet did I not bury myself alive in a nunnery, and triumph over love, at an age capable of enjoying it in its full latitude? 'Tis to you I sacrifice these remains of a transitory beauty, these widowed nights and tedious days which I pass without seeing you; and since you cannot possess them, I take them from you to offer them to Heaven, and to make, alas! but a secondary oblation of my heart, my days, and my life!

I am sensible I have dwelt too long on this head; I ought to speak less to you of your misfortunes, and of my own sufferings, for love of you. We tarnish the lustre of our most beautiful actions when we applaud them ourselves. This is true, and yet there is a time when we may with decency commend ourselves; when we have to do with those whom base ingratitude has stupefied, we cannot too much praise our own good actions. Now, if you were of this sort of men, this would be a home-reflection on you. Irresolute as I am, I still love you, and yet I must hope for nothing, I have renounced life, and stripped myself of every thing, but I find I neither have nor can renounce my *Abelard*. Though I have lost my lover, I still preserve my love. O vows! O convent! I have not lost my humanity under your inexorable discipline! You have not made me marble by changing my habit. My heart is not totally hardened by my perpetual imprisonment; I am still sensible to what has touched me, though, alas I ought not to be so. Without offending your commands, permit a lover to exhort me to live in obedience to your rigorous rules. Your yoke will be lighter, if that hand support me under it; your exercises will be amiable, if he shows me their advantage. Retirement, solitude! you will not appear terrible, if I may but still know I have any place in his memory. A heart which has been so sensibly affected as mine cannot soon be indifferent. We fluctuate long between love and hatred before we can arrive at a happy tranquillity, and we always flatter ourselves with some distant hope that we shall not be quite forgotten.

Yes, *Abelard*, I conjure you by the chains I bear here to ease the weight of them, and make them as agreeable as I wish they were to me. Teach me the maxims of divine love. Since you have forsaken me, I glory in being wedded to Heaven. My heart adores that title, and disdains any other. Tell me how this divine love is nourished, how it operates, and purifies itself. When we were tossed in the ocean of the world, we could hear of nothing but your verses, which published every where our joys and our pleasures: now we are in the haven of grace, is it not fit that you should discourse to me of this happiness, and teach me every thing which might improve and heighten it? Shew me the same complaisance in my present condition as you did when we were in the world. Without changing the ardour of our affections, let us change their object; let us leave our songs, and sing hymns; let us lift up our hearts to God, and have no transports but for his glory.

I expect this from you as a thing you cannot refuse me. God has a peculiar right over the hearts of great men which he has created. When he pleases to touch them, he ravishes them, and lets them not speak nor breathe but for his glory. Till that moment of grace arrives, O think of me——do not forget me;—remember my love, my fidelity, my constancy; love me as your mistress, cherish me as your child, your sister, your wife. Consider that I still love you, and yet strive to avoid loving you. What a word, what a design is this! I shake with horror, and my heart revolts against what I say. I shall blot all my paper with tears—I end my long letter, wishing you, if you can desire it, (would to Heaven I could,) for ever adieu.

Advertisement.

That the reader may make a right judgment on the following Letter, it is proper he should be informed of the condition *Abelard* was in when he wrote it. The Duke of Britany whose subject he was born, jealous of the glory of France, which then engrossed all the most famous scholars of Europe, and being, besides, acquainted with the persecution *Abelard* had suffered from his enemies, had nominated him to the Abbey of St. Gildas, and, by this benefaction and mark of his esteem, engaged him to past the rest of his days in his dominions. He received this favour with great joy, imagining, that by leaving France he should lose his passion, and gain a new turn of mind upon entering into his new dignity. The Abbey of St. Gildas is seated upon a rock, which the sea beats with its waves. *Abelard*, who had lain on himself the necessity of vanquishing a passion which absence had in a great measure weakened, endeavoured in this solitude to extinguish the remains of it by his tears. But upon his receiving the foregoing letter he could not resist so powerful an attack, but proves as weak and as much to be pitied as *Heloise*. 'Tis not then a master or director that speaks to her, but a man who had loved her, and loves her still: and under this character we are to consider *Abelard* when he wrote the following Letter. If he seems, by some passages in it, to have begun to feel the motions of divine grace they appear as yet to be only by starts, and without any uniformity.

Letter III. Abelard to Heloise.

Could I have imagined that a letter not written to yourself could have fallen into your hands, I had been more cautious not to have inserted any thing in it which might awaken the memory of our past misfortunes. I described with boldness the series of my disgraces to a friend, in order to make him less sensible of the loss he had sustained. If by this well meaning artifice I have disturbed you, I purpose here to dry up those tears which the sad description occasioned you to shed: I intend to mix my grief with yours, and pour out my heart before you; in short, to lay open before your eyes all my trouble, and the secrets of my soul, which my vanity has hitherto made me conceal from the rest of the world, and which you now force from me, in spite of my resolutions to the contrary.

It is true, that in a sense of the afflictions which had befallen us, and observing that no change of our condition was to be expected; that those prosperous days which had seduced us were now past, and there remained nothing but to eraze out of our minds, by painful endeavours, all marks and remembrance of them, I had wished to find in philosophy and religion a remedy for my disgrace; I searched out an asylum to secure me from love. I was come to the sad experiment of making vows to harden my heart. But what have I gained by this? If my passion has been put under a restraint, my ideas yet remain. I promise myself that I will forget you, and yet cannot think of it without loving you; and am pleased with that thought. My love is not at all weakened by those reflections I make in order to free myself. The silence I am surrounded with makes me more sensible to its impressions; and while I am unemployed with any other things, this makes itself the business of my whole vacation; till, after a multitude of useless endeavours, I begin to persuade myself that it is a superfluous trouble to drive to free myself; and that it is wisdom sufficient if I can conceal from every one but you my confusion and weakness.

I removed to a distance from your person, with an intention of avoiding you as an enemy; and yet I incessantly seek for you in my mind; I recall your image in my memory; and in such different disquietudes I betray and contradict myself. I hate you: I love you.

Shame presses me on all sides: I am at this moment afraid lest I should seem more indifferent than you, and yet I am ashamed to discover my trouble.

How weak are we in ourselves, if we do not support ourselves on the cross of Christ? Shall we have so little courage, and shall that uncertainty your heart labours with, of serving two masters, affect mine too? You see the confusion I am in, what I blame myself for, and what I suffer. Religion commands me to pursue virtue, since I have nothing to hope for from love. But love still preserves its dominion in my fancy, and entertains itself with past pleasures. Memory supplies the place of a mistress. Piety and duty are not always the fruits of retirement; even in deserts, when the dew of heaven falls not on us, we love what we ought no longer to love. The passions, stirred up by solitude, fill those regions of death and silence; and it is very seldom that what ought to be is truly followed there, and that God only is loved and served. Had I always had such notions as these, I had instructed you better. You call me your Master 'tis true, you were intrusted to my care. I saw you, I was earnest to teach you vain sciences; it cost you your innocence, and me my liberty. Your uncle, who was fond of you, became therefore me enemy, and revenge himself on me. If now, having lost the power of satisfying my passion, I had lost too that of loving you, I should have some consolation. My enemies would have given me that tranquillity which Origen purchased by a crime. How miserable am I! My misfortune does not loose my chains, my passion grows furious by impotence; and that desire I still have for you amidst all my disgraces makes me more unhappy than the misfortune itself. I find myself much more guilty in my thoughts of you, even amidst my tears, than in possessing yourself when I was in full liberty. I continually think of you, I continually call to mind that day when you bestowed on me the first marks of your tenderness. In this condition, O Lord! if I run to prostrate myself before thy altars, if I beseech thee to pity me, why does not the pure flame of thy Spirit consume the sacrifice that is offered to thee? Cannot this habit of penitence which I wear interest Heaven to treat me more favourably? But that is still inexorable; because my passion still lives in me, the fire is only covered over with deceitful ashes, and cannot be extinguished but by extraordinary graces. We deceive men, but nothing is hid from God.

Pierre Abelard

You tell me, that it is for me you live under that veil which covers you; why do you profane your vocation with such words? Why provoke a jealous God by a blasphemy? I hoped, after our separation, you would have changed your sentiments; I hoped too, that God would have delivered me from the tumult of my senses, and that contrariety which reigns in my heart. We commonly die to the affections of those whom we see no more, and they to ours: absence is the tomb of love. But to me absence is an unquiet remembrance of what I once loved, which continually torments me. I flattered myself, that when I should see you no more, you would only rest in my memory, without giving any trouble to my mind; that Britany and the sea would inspire other thoughts; that my fasts and studies would by degrees eraze you out of my heart; but in spite of severe fasts and redoubled studies, in spite of the distance of three hundred miles which separates us, your image, such as you describe yourself in your veil, appears to me, and confounds all my resolutions.

What means have I not used? I have armed my own hands against myself? I have exhausted my strength in constant exercises; I comment upon St. Paul; I dispute with Aristotle; in short, I do all I used to do before I loved you, but all in vain; nothing can be successful that opposes you. Oh! do not add to my miseries by your constancy; forget, if you can, your favours, and that right which they claim over me; permit me to be indifferent. I envy their happiness who have never loved; how quiet and easy are they! But the tide of pleasures has always a reflux of bitterness. I am but too much convinced now of this; but though I am no longer deceived by love, I am not cured: while my reason condemns it, my heart declares for it. I am deplorable that I have not the ability to free myself from a passion which so many circumstances, this place, my person, and my disgraces, tend to destroy. I yield, without considering that a resistance would wipe out my past offences, and would procure me in their stead merit and repose. Why should you use eloquence to reproach me for my flight, and for my silence? Spare the recital of our assignations, and your constant exactness to them; without calling up such disturbing thoughts, I have enough to suffer. What great advantages would philosophy give us over other men, if by studying it we could learn to govern our passions? but how humbled ought we to be when we cannot master them? What efforts, what relapses, what agitations, do we undergo? and how long are we tossed in this confusion, unable to exert our reason, to possess our souls, or to rule our affections?

What a troublesome employment is love! and how valuable is virtue even upon consideration of our own ease! Recoiled your extravagances of passion, guess at my distractions: number up our cares, if possible, our griefs, and our inquietudes; throw these things out of the account, and let love have all its remaining softness and pleasure. How little is that? and, yet for such shadows of enjoyments, which at first appeared to us, are we so weak our whole lives that we cannot now help writing to each other, covered as we are with sackcloth and ashes! How much happier should we be, if, by our humiliation and tears, we could make our repentance sure! The love of pleasure is not eradicated out of the soul but by extraordinary efforts; it has so powerful a party in our breasts, that we find it difficult to condemn it ourselves. What abhorrence can I be said to have of my sins, if the objects of them are always amiable to me? How can I separate from the person I love the passion I must detest? Will the tears I shed be sufficient to render it odious to me? I know not how it happens, there is always a pleasure in weeping for a beloved object. 'Tis difficult in our sorrow to distinguish penitence from love. The memory of the crime, and the memory of the object which has charmed us, are too nearly related to be immediately separated: and the love of God in its beginning does not wholly annihilate the love of the creature. But what excuses could I not find in you, if the crime were excusable? Unprofitable honour, troublesome riches, could never tempt me; but those charms, that beauty, that air, which I yet behold at this instant, have occasioned my fall. Your looks were the beginning of my guilt; your eyes, your discourse, pierced my heart; and in spite of that ambition and glory which filled it, and offered to make defence, love soon made itself master. God, in order to punish me, forsook me. His providence permitted those consequences which have since happened. You are no longer of the world; you have renounced it; I am a Religious, devoted to solitude; shall we make no advantage of our condition? Would you destroy my piety in its infant-state? Would you have me forsake the convent into which I am but newly entered? Must I renounce my vows? I have made them in the presence of God; whither shall I fly from his wrath if I violate them? Suffer me to seek for ease in my duty; how difficult it is to procure that! I pass whole days and nights alone in this cloister, without closing my eyes. My love burns fiercer, amidst the happy indifference of those who surround me, and my heart is at once pierced with your sorrows and its own. Oh what a loss have I sustained, when I consider your constancy! What pleasures have I missed enjoying! I ought not to confess this weakness to you: I am sensible I commit a fault: if I could have showed more firmness of mind, I should, perhaps, have provoked your resentment against me, and your anger might work that effect in you which your virtue could not. If in the world I published my weakness by verses and love-songs, ought not the dark cells of this house to conceal that weakness, at least, under an appearance of piety? Alas! I am still the same! or if I avoid the evil, I cannot do the good; and yet I ought to join both, in order to make this manner of living profitable. But how difficult is this in the trouble which surrounds me? Duty, reason, and decency, which, upon other occasions have such power over me, are here entirely useless. The gospel is a language I do not understand, when it opposes my passion. Those oaths which I have taken before the holy altar, are feeble helps when opposed to you. Amidst so many voices which call me to my duty, I hear and obey nothing but the secret dictates of a desperate passion. Void of all relish for virtue, any concern for my condition, or any application to my studies, I am continually present by my imagination where I ought not to be, and I find I have no power, when I would at any time correct it. I feel a perpetual strife between my inclination and my duty. I find myself entirely a distracted lover; unquiet in the midst of silence, and restless in this abode of peace and repose. How shameful is such a condition!

Consider me no more, I intreat you, as a founder, or any great personage; your encomiums do but ill agree with such multiplied weaknesses. I am a miserable sinner, prostrate before my Judge, and, with my face pressed to the earth, I mix my tears and my sighs in the dust, when the beams of grace and reason enlighten me. Come, see me in this posture, and solicit me to love you! Come, if you think fit, and in your holy habit thrust yourself between God and me and be a wall of separation! Come, and force from me those sighs, thoughts, and vows, which I owe to him only. Assist the evil spirits, and be the instrument of their malice. What cannot you induce a heart to, whose weakness you so perfectly know? But rather withdraw yourself, and contribute to my salvation. Suffer me to avoid destruction, I intreat you, by our former tenderest affection, and by our common misfortune. It will always be the highest love to show none. I here release you of all your oaths and engagements. Be God's wholly, to whom you are appropriated; I will never oppose so pious a design. How happy shall I be if I thus lose you! then shall I be indeed a Religious, and you a perfect example of an Abbess.

Make yourself amends by so glorious a choice; make your virtue a spectacle worthy men and angels: be humble among your children, assiduous in your choir, exact in your discipline, diligent in your reading; make even your recreations useful. Have you purchased your vocation at so slight a rate, as that you should not turn it to the best advantage? Since you have permitted yourself to be abused by false doctrine, and criminal instructions, resist not those good-counsels which grace and religion inspire me with. I will confess to you, I have thought myself hitherto an abler master to instill vice than to excite virtue, My false eloquence has only set off false good. My heart drunk with voluptuousness, could only suggest terms proper and moving to recommend that. The cup of sinners overflows with so inchanting a sweetness and we are naturally so much inclined to taste it, that it needs only be offered to us. On the other hand, the chalice of saints is filled with a bitter draught, and nature starts from it. And yet you reproach me with cowardice for giving it you first; I willingly submit to these accusations. I cannot enough admire the readiness you showed to take the religious habit: bear, therefore, with courage the Cross, which you have taken up so resolutely. Drink of the chalice of saints, even to the bottom, without turning your eyes with uncertainty upon me, Let me remove far from you, and obey the apostle, who hath said, *Fly.*

You intreat me to return, under a pretence of devotion, Your earnestness in this point creates a suspicion in me, and makes me doubtful how to answer you. Should I commit an error here, my words would blush, if I may say so, after the history of my misfortunes. The Church is jealous of its glory, and commands that her children should be induced to the practice of virtue by virtuous means. When we have approached God after an unblameable manner, we may then with boldness invite others to him. But to forget *Heloise*, to see her no more, is what Heaven demands of *Abelard*; and to expect nothing from *Abelard*, to lose him even in idea, is what Heaven enjoins *Heloise*. To forget in the case of love is the most necessary penitence, and the most difficult. It is easy to recount our faults. How many through indiscretion have made themselves a second pleasure of this, instead of confessing them with humility. The only way to return to God is, by neglecting the creature which we have adored, and adoring God whom we have neglected. This may appear harsh, but it must be done if we would be saved.

To make it more easy, observe why I pressed you to your vow before I took mine; and pardon my sincerity, and the design I have of meriting your neglect and hatred, if I conceal nothing from you of the particular you inquire after. When I saw myself so oppressed with my misfortune, my impotency made me jealous, and I considered all men as my rivals. Love has more of distrust than assurance. I was apprehensive of abundance of things, because I saw I had abundance of defects; and being tormented with fear from my own example, I imagined your heart, which had been so much accustomed to love, would not be long without entering into a new engagement. Jealousy can easily believe to most dreadful consequences, I was desirous to put myself out of a possibility of doubting you. I was very urgent to persuade you, that decency required you should withdraw from the envious eyes of the world; that modesty, and our friendship, demanded it; nay, that your own safety obliged you to it; and, that after such a revenge taken upon me, you could expect to be secure no where but in a convent.

I will do you justice; you were very easily persuaded to it. My jealousy secretly triumphed over your innocent compliance; and yet, triumphant as I was, I yielded you up to God with an unwilling heart. I still kept my gift as much as was possible, and only parted with it that I might effectually put it out of the power of men. I did not persuade you to religion out of any regard to your happiness, but condemned you to it, like an enemy who destroys what he cannot carry off. And yet you heard my discourses with kindness; you sometimes interrupted me with tears, and pressed me to acquaint you which of the convents was most in my esteem. What a comfort did I feel in seeing you shut up! I was now at ease, and took a satisfaction in considering that you did not continue long in the world after my disgrace, and that you would return into it no more.

But still this was doubtful. I imagined women were incapable of maintaining any constant resolutions, unless they were forced by the necessity of fixed vows. I wanted those vows, and Heaven itself, for your security, that I might no longer distrust you. Ye holy mansions, ye impenetrable retreats, from what numberless apprehensions have you freed me? Religion and Piety keep a strict guard round your grates and high walls. What a haven of rest is this to a jealous mind? and with what impatience did I endeavour it! I went every day trembling to exhort you to this sacrifice; I admired, without daring to mention it then, a brightness in your beauty which I had never observed before. Whether it was the bloom of a rising virtue, or an anticipation of that great loss I was going to suffer, I was not curious in examining the cause, but only hastened your being professed. I engaged your Prioress in my guilt by a criminal bribe, with which I purchased the right of burying you. The professed of the house were also bribed, and concealed from you, by my directions, all their scruples and disgusts. I omitted nothing, either little or great: and if you had escaped all my snares, I myself would not have retired: I was resolved to follow you every where. This shadow of myself would always have pursued your steps, and continually occasioned either your confusion or fear, which would have been a sensible gratification to me.

But, thanks to Heaven, you resolved to make a vow; I accompanied you with terror to the foot of the altar: and while you stretched out your hand to touch the sacred cloth, I heard you pronounce distinctly those fatal words which for ever separated you from all men. 'Till then your beauty and youth seemed to oppose my design, and to threaten your return into the world. Might not a small temptation have changed you? Is it possible to renounce one's self entirely at the age of two and twenty? at an age which claims the most absolute liberty, could you think the world no longer worthy of your regard? How much did I wrong you, and what weakness did I impute to you? You were in my imagination nothing but lightness and inconstancy. Might not a young woman, at the noise of the flames, and the fall of Sodom, look back, and pity some one person? I took notice of your eyes, your motion, your air; I trembled at every thing. You may call such a self-interested conduct treachery, perfidiousness, murder. A love which was so like to hatred ought to provoke the utmost contempt and anger.

It is fit you should know, that the very moment when I was convinced of your being entirely devoted to me, when I saw you were infinitely worthy of all my love and acknowledgement, I imagined I could love you no more; I thought it time to leave off giving you any marks of affection; and I considered, that by your holy espousals you were now the peculiar care of Heaven, even in the quality of a wife. My jealousy seemed to be extinguished. When God only is our rival, we have nothing to fear: and being in greater tranquillity than ever before, I dared even to offer up prayers, and beseech him to take you away from my eyes: but it was not a time to make rash prayers; and my faith was too imperfect to let them be heard. He who sees the depth and secrets of all men's hearts, saw mine did not agree with my words. Necessity and despair were the springs of this proceeding. Thus I inadvertently offered an insult to Heaven rather than a sacrifice. God rejected my offering and my prayers, and continued my punishment, by suffering me to continue my love. Thus, under the guilt of your vows, and of the passion which preceded them, I must be tormented all the days of my life.

If God spoke to your heart, as to that of a Religious, whose innocence had first engaged him to heap on it a thousand favours, I should have matter of comfort; but to see both of us victims of a criminal love; to see this love insult us, and invest itself with our very habits, as with spoils it has taken from our devotion, fills me with horror and trembling. Is this a state of reprobation? or are these the consequences of a long drunkenness in profane love? We cannot say love is a drunkenness and a poison till we are illuminated by grace; in the mean time, it is an evil which we dote on. When we are under such a mistake the knowledge of our misery is the first step towards amendment. Who does not know that it is for the glory of God to find no other foundation in man for his mercy than man's very weakness? When he has shewed us this weakness, and we bewail it, he is ready to put forth his omnipotence to assist us. Let us say for our comfort that what we suffer is one of those long and terrible temptations which have sometimes disturbed the vocations of the most Holy.

God can afford his presence to men, in order to soften their calamities, whenever he shall think fit. It was his pleasure when you took the veil, to draw you to him by his grace. I saw your eyes, when you spoke your last farewell, fixed upon the cross. It was above six months before you wrote me a letter, nor during all that time did I receive any message from you. I admired this silence, which I durst not blame, and could not imitate. I wrote to you; you returned me no answer. Your heart was then shut; but this guardian of the spouse is now opened, he is withdrawn from it, and has left you alone. By removing from you, he has made trial of you; call him back and strive to regain him. We must have the assistance of God that we may break our chains; we have engaged too deeply in love to free ourselves. Our follies have penetrated even into the most sacred places. Our amours have been matter of scandal to a whole kingdom. They are read and admired; love which produced them has caused them to be described. We shall be a consolation for the failings of youth hereafter. Those who offend after us will think themselves less guilty. We are criminals whose repentance is late. O may it be sincere! Let us repair, as far is possible, the evils we have done; and let France, which has been the witness of our crimes, be astonished at our penitence. Let us confound all who would imitate our guilt, let us take the part of God against ourselves, and by so doing prevent his judgment. Our former irregularities require tears, shame, and sorrow to expiate them. Let us offer up these sacrifices from our hearts; let us blush, let us weep. If in these weak beginnings, Lord, our heart is not entirely thine, let it at least be made sensible that it ought to be so!

Deliver yourself, *Heloise*, from the shameful remains of a passion which has taken too deep root. Remember that the least thought for any other than God is adultery. If you could see me here, with my meagre face and melancholy air, surrounded with numbers of persecuting monks, who are alarmed at my reputation for learning, and offended at my lean visage, as if I threatened them with a reformation; what would you say of my base sighs, and of those unprofitable tears which deceive these credulous men? Alas! I am humbled under love, and not under the Cross. Pity me, and free yourself. If your vocation be, as you say, my work, deprive me not of the merit of it by your continual inquietudes. Tell me that you, will honour the habit which covers you, by an inward retirement. Fear God, that you may be delivered from your frailties. Love him, if you would advance in virtue. Be not uneasy in the cloister, for it is the dwelling of saints. Embrace your bands, they are the chains of Christ Jesus: he will lighten them, and bear them with you, if you bear them with humility.

Without growing severe to a passion which yet possesses you, learn from your own misery to succour your weak sisters; pity them upon consideration of your own faults. And if any thoughts too natural shall importune you, fly to the foot of the Cross, and beg for mercy; there are wounds open; lament before the dying Deity. At the head of a religious society be not a slave, and having rule over queens, begin to govern yourself. Blush at the least revolt of your senses. Remember, that even at the foot of the altar we often sacrifice to lying spirits, and that no incense can be more agreeable to them than that which in those places burns in the heart of a Religious still sensible of passion and love. If, during your abode in the world, your soul has acquired a habit of loving, feel it now no more but for Jesus Christ, Repent of all the moments of your life which you have wasted upon the world, and upon pleasure; demand them of me, it is a robbery which I am guilty of; take courage and boldly reproach me with it.

I have been indeed your master, but it was only to teach you sin. You call me your Father; before I had any claim to this title I deserved that of Parricide. I am your brother, but it is the affinity of our crimes that has purchased me that distinction. I am called your Husband, but it is after a public scandal. If you have abused the sanctity of so many venerable names in the superscription of your letters, to do me honour, and flatter your own passion, blot them out, and place in their stead those of a Murtherer, a Villain, an Enemy, who has conspired against your honour, troubled your quiet, and betrayed your innocence. You would have perished thro' my means, but by an extraordinary act of grace, which that you might be saved, has thrown me down in the middle of my course.

This is the idea that you ought to have of a fugitive, who endeavours to deprive you of the hope of seeing him any more. But when love has once been sincere, how difficult it is to determine to love no more? 'Tis a thousand times more easy to renounce the world than love. I hate this deceitful faithless world; I think no more of it; but my heart, still wandering, will eternally make me feel the anguish of having lost you, in spite of all the convictions of my understanding. In the mean time tho' I so be so cowardly as to retract what you have read, do not suffer me to offer myself to your thoughts but under this last notion. Remember my last endeavours were to seduce your heart. You perished by my means, and I with you. The same waves swallowed us both up. We waited for death with indifference, and the same death had carried us headlong to the same punishments. But Providence has turned off this blow, and our shipwreck has thrown us into an haven. There are some whom the mercy of God saves by afflictions. Let my salvation be the fruit of your prayers! let me owe it to your tears, or exemplary holiness! Tho' my heart, Lord! be filled with the love of one of thy creatures, thy hand can, when it pleases, draw out of it those ideas which fill its whole capacity. To love *Heloise* truly is to leave her entirely to that quiet which retirement and virtue afford. I have resolved it: this letter shall be my last fault. Adieu.

If I die here, I will give orders that my body be carried to the house of the Paraclete. You shall see me in that condition; not to demand tears from you, it will then be too late; weep rather for me now, to extinguish that fire which burns me. You shall see me, to strengthen your piety by the horror of this carcase; and my death, then more eloquent than I can be, will tell you what you love when you love a man. I hope you will be contented, when you have finished this mortal life, to be buried near me. Your cold ashes need then fear nothing, and my tomb will, by that means, be more rich and more renowned.

Letter IV. Heloise to Abelard.

In the following Letter the passion of *Heloise* breaks, out with more violence than ever. That which she had received from *Abelard*, instead of fortifying her resolutions, served only to revive in her memory all their past endearments and misfortunes. With this impression she writes again to her husband; and appears now, not so much in the charter of a Religious, striving with the remains of her former weakness, as in that of an unhappy woman abandoned to all the transport of love and despair.

To *Abelard*, her well beloved in Christ Jesus, from *Heloise*, his well-beloved, in the same Christ Jesus.

I read the letter I received from you with abundance of impatience. In spite of all my misfortunes, I hoped to find nothing in it besides arguments of comfort; but how ingenious are lovers in tormenting themselves! Judge of the exquisite sensibility and force of my love by that which causes the grief of my soul; I was disturbed at the superscription of your letter! why did you place the name of *Heloise* before that of *Abelard*? what means this most cruel and unjust distinction? 'Twas your name only, the name of Father, and of a Husband, which my eager eyes sought after. I did not look for my own, which I much rather, if possible, forget, as being the cause of your misfortune. The rules of decorum, and the character of Master and Director which you have over me, opposed that ceremonious manner of addressing me; and Love commanded you to banish it. Alas! you know all this but too well.

Did you write thus to me before Fortune had ruined my happiness? I see your heart has deserted me, and you have made greater advances in the way of devotion than I could wish. Alas! I am too weak to follow you; condescend at least to stay for me, and animate me with your advice. Will you have the cruelty to abandon me? The fear of this stabs my heart: but the fearful presages you make at the latter end of your Letter, those terrible images you draw of your death, quite distracts me. Cruel *Abelard*! you ought to have stopped my tears, and you make them flow; you ought to have quieted the disorder of my heart, and you throw me into despair.

You desire that after your death I should take care of your ashes, and pay them the last duties. Alas! in what temper did you conceive these mournful ideas? and how could you describe them to me? Did not the apprehension of causing my present death make the pen drop from your hand? You did not reflect, I suppose, upon all those' torments to which you were going to deliver me. Heaven, as severe as it has been against me, is not in so great a degree so, as to permit me to live one moment after you. Life without my *Abelard* is an unsupportable punishment, and death a most exquisite happiness, if by that means I can be united with him. If Heaven hears the prayers I continually make for you, your days will be prolonged, and you will bury me.

Is it not your part to prepare me, by your powerful exhortations against that great crisis, which shakes the most resolute and confirmed minds? Is it not your part to receive my last sighs; take care of my funeral, and give an account of my manners and faith? Who but you can recommend us worthily to God; and by the fervour and merit of your prayers, conduct those souls to him which you have joined to his worship by solemn contracts? We expect these pious offices from your paternal charity. After this you will be free from those disquietudes which now molest you, and you will quit life with more ease, whenever it shall please God to call you away. You may follow us, content with what you have done, and in a full assurance of our happiness: but till then, write not to me any such terrible things. Are we not already sufficiently miserable? must we aggravate our sorrows? Our life here is but a languishing death? will you hasten it? Our present disgraces are sufficient to employ our thoughts continually, and shall we seek new arguments of grief in futurities? How void of reason are men, said Seneca, to make distant evils present by reflection, and to take pains before death to lose all the comforts of life?

When you have finished your course here below, you say it is your desire that your body be carried to the house of the Paraclete, to the intent that, being always exposed to my eyes, you may be for ever present to my mind; and that your dear body may strengthen our piety, and animate our prayers. Can you think that the traces you have drawn in my heart can ever be worn out? or that any length of time can obliterate the memory we have here of your benefits? And what time shall I find for those prayers you speak of? Alas! I shall then be filled with other cares. Can so heavy a misfortune leave me a moment's quiet? can my feeble reason resist such powerful assaults? When I am distracted and raving, (if I dare to say it,) even against Heaven itself, I shall not soften it by my prayers, but rather provoke it by my cries and reproaches! But how should I pray! or how bear up against my grief? I should be more urgent to follow you than to pay you the sad ceremonies of burial. It is for you for *Abelard*, that I have resolved to live; if you are ravished from me, what use can I make of my miserable days? Alas! what lamentations should I make, if Heaven, by a cruel pity, should preserve me till that moment? When I but think of this last separation; I feel all the pangs of death; what shall I be then, if I should see this dreadful hour? Forbear, therefore, to infuse into my mind such mournful thoughts, if not for love, at least for pity.

You desire me to give myself up to my duty, and to be wholly God's, to whom I am consecrated. How can I do that when you frighten me with apprehensions that continually possess my mind day and night? When an evil threatens us, and it is impossible to ward it off, why do we give up ourselves to the unprofitable fear of it, which is yet even more tormenting than the evil itself?

What have I to hope for after this loss of you? what can confine me to earth when Death shall have taken away from me all that was dear upon it? I have renounced without difficulty all the charms of life, preserving only my love, and the secret pleasure of thinking incessantly of you, and hearing that you live; and yet alas! you do not live for me, and I dare not even flatter myself with the hopes that I shall ever enjoy a sight of you more. This is the greatest of my afflictions. Merciless Fortune! hast thou not persecuted me enough? Thou dost not give me any respite? thou hast exhausted all thy vengeance upon me, and reserved thyself nothing whereby thou mayst appear terrible to others. Thou hast wearied thyself in tormenting me, and others have nothing now to fear from thy anger. But to what purpose dost thou still arm thyself against me? The wounds I have already received leave no room for new ones; why cannot I urge thee to kill me? or dost thou fear, amidst the numerous torments thou heapest on me, dost thou fear that such a stroke would deliver me from all? Therefore thou preservest me from death, in order to make me die every moment.

Dear *Abelard*, pity my despair! Was ever any thing so miserable! The higher you raised me above other women who envied me your love, the more sensible am I now of the loss of your heart. I was exalted to the top of happiness, only that I might have a more terrible fall. Nothing could formerly be compared to my pleasures, and nothing now can equal my misery. My glory once raised the envy of my rivals; my present wretchedness moves the compassion of all that see me. My fortune has been always in extremes, she has heaped on me her most delightful favours, that she might load me with the greatest of her afflictions. Ingenious in tormenting me, she has made the memory of the joys I have lost, an inexhaustible spring of my tears. Love, which possest was her greatest gift, being taken away, occasions all my sorrow. In short, her malice has entirely succeeded, and I find my present afflictions proportionably bitter as the transports which charmed me were sweet.

But what aggravates my sufferings yet more, is, that we began to be miserable at a time when we seemed the least to deserve it. While we gave ourselves up to the enjoyment of a criminal love, nothing opposed our vicious pleasures. But scarce had we retrenched what was unlawful in our passion, and taken refuge in marriage against that remorse which might have pursued us, but the whole wrath of heaven fell on us in all its weight. But how barbarous was your punishment? The very remembrance makes me shake with horror. Could an outrageous husband make a villain suffer more that had dishonoured his bed? Ah! What right had a cruel uncle over us? We were joined to each other even before the altar, which should have protected you from the rage of your enemies. Must a wife draw on you that punishment which ought not to fall on any but an adulterous lover? Besides, we were separated; you were busy in your exercises, and instructed a learned auditory in mysteries which the greatest geniuses before you were not able to penetrate; and I, in obedience to you, retired to a cloister. I there spent whole days in thinking of you, and sometimes meditating on holy lessons, to which I endeavoured to apply myself. In this very juncture you became the victim of the most unhappy love. You alone expiated the crime common to us both: You only were punished, though both of us were guilty. You, who were least so, was the object of the whole vengeance of a barbarous man.

But why should I rave at your assassins? I, wretched I, have ruined you, I have been the original of all your misfortunes! Good Heaven! Why was I born to be the occasion of so tragical an accident? How dangerous is it for a great man to suffer himself to be moved by our sex! He ought from his infancy to be inured to insensibility of heart, against all our charms. *Hearken, my Son,* (said formerly the wisest of Men) *attend and keep my instructions; if a beautiful woman by her looks endeavour to intice thee, permit not thyself to be overcome by a corrupt inclination; reject the poison she offers, and follow not the paths which she directs. Her house is the gate of destruction and death.* I have long examined things, and have found that death itself is a less dangerous evil than beauty. 'Tis the shipwreck of liberty, a fatal snare, from which it is impossible ever to get free. 'Twas woman which threw down the first man from that glorious condition in which heaven had placed him. She who was created in order to partake of his happiness, was the sole cause of his ruin. How bright had been the glory, *Sampson,* if thy heart had been as firm against the charms of *Dalilah,* as against the weapons of the *Philistines*! A woman disarmed and betrayed thee, who hadst been a glorious conqueror of armies. Thou saw'st thyself delivered into the hands of they enemies; thou wast deprived of thy eyes, those inlets of love into thy soul: distracted and despairing didst thou die, without any consolation but that of involving thy enemies in thy destruction. *Solomon,* that he might please women, forsook the care of pleasing God. That king, whose wisdom princes came from all parts to admire, he whom God had chose to build him a temple, abandoned the worship of those very alters he had had defended, and proceeded to such a pitch of folly as even to burn incense to idols. *Job* had no enemy more cruel than his wife: what temptations did he not bear? The evil spirit, who had declared himself his persecutor, employed a woman as an instrument to shake his constancy; and the same evil spirit made *Heloise* an instrument to ruin *Abelard*! All the poor comfort I have is, that I am not the voluntary cause of your misfortune. I have not betrayed you; but my constancy and love have been destructive to you. If I have committed a crime in having loved you with constancy, I shall never be able to repent of that crime. Indeed I gave myself up too much to the captivity of those soft errors into which my rising passion seduced me. I have endeavoured to please you even at the expence of my virtue, and therefore deserve those pains I feel. My guilty transports could not but have a tragical end. As soon as I was persuaded of your love, alas! I scarce delayed a moment, resigning myself to all your protestations. To be beloved by *Abelard* was, in my esteem, too much glory, and I too impatiently desired it not to believe it immediately. I endeavoured at nothing but convincing you of my utmost passion. I made no use of those defences of disdain and honour; those enemies of pleasure which tyrannize over our sex, made in me but a weak and unprofitable resistance. I sacrificed all to my love, and I forced my duty to give place to the ambition of making happy the most gallant and learned person of the age. If any consideration had been able to stop me, it would have been without doubt the interest of my love. I feared, lest having nothing further for you to desire, your passion might become languid, and you might seek for new pleasures in some new conquest. But it was easy for you to cure me of a suspicion so opposite to my own inclination. I ought to have forseen other more certain evils, and to have considered, that the idea of lost enjoyments would be the trouble of my whole life.

How happy should I be could I wash out with my tears the memory of those pleasures which yet I think of with delight? At least I will exert some generous endeavour, and, by smothering in my heart those desires to which the frailty of my nature may give birth, I will exercise torments upon myself, like those the rage of your enemies has made you suffer. I will endeavour by that means to satisfy you at least, if I cannot appease an angry God. For, to show you what a deplorable condition I am in, and how far my repentance is from being available, I dare even accuse Heaven every moment of cruelty for delivering you into those snares which were prepared for you. My repinings kindle the divine wrath, when I should endeavour to draw down mercy.

In order to expiate a crime, it is not sufficient that we bear the punishment; whatever we suffer is accounted as nothing, if the passions still continue, and the heart is inflamed with the same desires. It is an easy matter to confess a weakness, and to inflict some punishment upon ourselves; but it is the last violence to our nature to extinguish the memory of pleasures which, by a sweet habit, have gained absolute possession of our minds. How many persons do we observe who make an outward confession of their faults, yet, far from being afflicted for them, take a new pleasure in the relating them. Bitterness of heart ought to accompany the confession of the mouth, yet that very rarely happens. I, who have experienced so many pleasures in loving you, feel, in spite of myself that I cannot repent of them, nor forbear enjoying them over again as much as is possible, by recollecting them in my memory. Whatever endeavours I use, on whatever side I turn me, the sweet idea still pursues me and every object brings to my mind what I ought to forget. During the still night, when my heart ought to be in quiet in the midst of sleep, which suspends the greatest disturbances, I cannot avoid those illusions my heart entertains. I think I am still with my dear *Abelard*. I see him, I speak to him, and hear him answer. Charmed with each other, we quit our philosophic studies to entertain ourselves with our passion. Sometimes, too, I seem to be a witness of the bloody enterprise of your enemies; I oppose their fury; I fill our apartment with fearful cries, and in a moment I wake in tears. Even in holy places before the altar I carry with me the memory of our guilty loves. They are my whole business, and, far from lamenting for having been seduced, I sigh for having lost them.

I remember (for nothing is forgot by lovers) the time and place in which you first declared your love to me, and swore you would love me till death. Your words, your oaths, are all deeply graven in my heart. The disorder of my discourse discovers to everyone the trouble of my mind. My sighs betray me; and your name is continually in my mouth. When I am in this condition, why dost not thou, O Lord, pity my weakness, and strengthen me by thy grace? You are happy, *Abelard*; this grace has prevented you; and your misfortune has been the occasion of your finding rest. The punishment of your body has cured the deadly wounds of your soul. The tempest has driven you into the haven. God who seemed to lay his hand heavily upon you, fought only to help you: he is a father chastising, and not an enemy revenging; a wife physician, putting you to some pain in order to preserve your life. I am a thousand times more to be lamented than you; I have a thousand passions to combat with. I must resist those fires which Jove kindles in a young heart. Our sex is nothing but weakness, and I have the greater difficulty to defend myself, because the enemy that attacks me pleases. I dote on the danger which threatens me, how then can I avoid falling?

In the midst of these struggles I endeavour at least to conceal my weakness from those you have entrusted to my care. All who are about me admired my virtue, but could their eyes penetrate into my heart, what would they not discover? My passions there are in a rebellion; I preside over others, but cannot rule myself. I have but a false covering, and this seeming virtue is a real vice. Men judge me praise-worthy, but I am guilty before God, from whose all-seeing eye nothing is hid, and who views, through all their foldings, the secrets of all hearts. I cannot escape his discovery. And yet it is a great deal to me to maintain even this appearance of virtue. This troublesome hypocrisy is in some sort commendable. I give no scandal to the world, which is so easy to take bad impressions. I do not shake the virtue of these feeble ones who are under my conduct. With my heart full of the love of man, I exhort them at least to love only God: charmed with the pomp of worldly pleasures, I endeavour to show them that they are all deceit and vanity. I have just strength enough to conceal from them my inclinations, and I look upon that as a powerful effect of grace. If it is not sufficient to make me embrace virtue, it is enough to keep me from committing sin.

And yet it is in vain to endeavour to separate those two things. They must be guilty who merit nothing; and they depart from virtue who delay to approach it. Besides, we ought to have no other motive than the love of God. Alas! what can I then hope for? I own, to my confusion, I fear more the offending of man than the provoking of God, and study less to please him than you. Yes, it was your command only, and not a sincere vocation, as is imagined, that shut me up in these cloisters. I fought to give you ease, and not to sanctify myself. How unhappy am I? I tear myself from all that pleases me? I bury myself here alive, I exercise my self in the most rigid fastings; and such severities as cruel laws impose on us; I feed myself with tears and sorrows, and, notwithstanding this, I deserve nothing for all the hardships I suffer. My false piety has long deceived you as well as others. You have thought me easy, and yet I was more disturbed than ever. You persuaded yourself I was wholly taken up with my duty, yet I had no business but love. Under this mistake you desire my prayers; alas! I must expect yours. Do not presume upon my virtue and my care. I am wavering, and you must fix me by your advice. I am yet feeble, you must sustain and guide me by your counsel.

What occasion had you to praise me? praise is often hurtful to those on whom it is bestowed. A secret vanity springs up in the heart, blinds us, and conceals from us wounds that are ill cured. A seducer flatters us, and at the same time, aims at our destruction. A sincere friend disguises nothing from us, and from passing a light hand over the wound, makes us feel it the more intensely, by applying remedies. Why do you not deal after this manner with me? Will you be

~ 83 ~

esteemed a base dangerous flatterer; or, if you chance to see any thing commendable in me, have you no fear that vanity, which is so natural to all women, should quite efface it? but let us not judge of virtue by outward appearances, for then the reprobates as well as the elect may lay claim to it. An artful impostor may, by his address gain more admiration than the true zeal of a saint.

The heart of man is a labyrinth, whose windings are very difficult to be discovered. The praises you give me are the more dangerous, in regard that I love the person who gives them. The more I desire to please you, the readier am I to believe all the merit you attribute to me. Ah, think rather how to support my weaknesses by wholesome remonstrances! Be rather fearful than confident of my salvation: say our virtue is founded upon weakness, and that those only will be crowned who have fought with the greatest difficulties: but I seek not for that crown which is the reward of victory, I am content to avoid only the danger. It is easier to keep off than to win a battle. There are several degrees in glory, and I am not ambitious of the highest; those I leave to souls of great courage, who have been often victorious. I seek not to conquer, out of fear lest I should be overcome. Happy enough, if I can escape shipwreck, and at last gain the port. Heaven commands me to renounce that fatal passion which unites me to you; but oh! my heart will never be able to consent to it. Adieu.

Letter V. Heloise to Abelard.

Heloise had been dangerously ill at the Convent of the Paraclete: immediately upon her recovery she wrote this Letter to *Abelard*, She seems now to have disengaged herself from him, and to have resolved to think of nothing but repentance; yet discovers some emotions, which make it doubtful whether devotion had entirely triumphed over her passion.

Dear *Abelard*, you expect, perhaps, that I should accuse you of negligence. You have not answered my last letter; and thanks to Heaven, in the condition I now am, it is a happiness to me that you show so much insensibility for the fatal passion which had engaged me to you. At last *Abelard*, you have lost *Heloise* for ever. Notwithstanding all the oaths I made to think of nothing but you only, and to be entertained with nothing but you, I have banished you from my thoughts, I have forgot you. Thou charming idea of a lover I once adored, thou wilt no more be my happiness! Dear image of *Abelard*! thou wilt no more follow me every where; I will no more remember thee. O celebrated merit of a man, who, in spite of his enemies is the wonder of his age! O enchanting pleasures, to which *Heloise* entirely resigned herself, you, you have been my tormentors! I confess *Abelard*, without a blush, my infidelity; let my inconstancy teach the world that there is no depending upon the promises of women; they are all subject to change. This troubles you, *Abelard*; this news, without doubt, surprises you; you could never imagine *Heloise*, should be inconstant. She was prejudiced by so strong an inclination to you, that you cannot conceive how time could alter it. But be undeceived; I am going to discover to you my falseness, though instead of reproaching me, I persuade myself you will shed tears of joy. When I shall have told you what rival hath ravished my heart from you, you will praise my inconstancy, and will pray this rival to fix it. By this you may judge that it is God alone that takes *Heloise* from you. Yes, my dear *Abelard*, he gives my mind that tranquillity which a quick remembrance of our misfortunes would not suffer me to enjoy. Just Heaven! what other rival could take me from you? Could you imagine it possible for any mortal to blot you from my heart? Could you think me guilty of sacrificing the virtuous and learned *Abelard* to any other but to God? No, I believe you have done me justice in this point. I question not but you are impatient to know what means God used to accomplish so great an end; I will tell you, and wonder at the secret ways of Providence. Some few days after you sent me your last letter I fell dangerously ill; the physicians gave me over; and I expected certain death. Then it was that my passion, which always before seemed innocent, appeared criminal to me. My memory represented faithfully to me all the past actions of my life, and I confess to you my love was the only pain I felt. Death which till then I had always considered as at a distance, now presented itself to me such as it appears to sinners. I began to dread the wrath of God, now I was going to experience it; and I repented I had made no better use of his grace. Those tender letters I have wrote to you, and those passionate conversations I have had with you, gave me as much pain now as they formerly did pleasure. Ah! miserable *Heloise*, said I, if it is a crime to give one's self up to such soft transports, and if after this life is ended punishment certainly follows them, why didst thou not resist so dangerous an inclination? Think on the tortures that are prepared for thee; consider with terror that store of torments, and recollect at the same time those pleasures which thy deluded soul thought so entrancing. Ah! pursued I, dost thou not almost despair for having rioted in such false pleasure? In short, *Abelard*, imagine all the remorse of mind I suffered, and you will not be astonished at my change.

Solitude is insupportable to a mind which is not easy, its troubles increase in the midst of silence, and retirement heightens them. Since I have been shut up within these walls, I have done nothing but wept for our misfortunes. This cloister has resounded with my cries, and like a wretch condemned to eternal slavery, I have worn out my days in grief and sighing. Instead of fulfilling God's merciful design upon me, I have offended him; I have looked upon this sacred refuge like a frightful prison, and have borne with unwillingness the yoke of the Lord. Instead of sanctifying myself by a life of penitence, I have confirmed my reprobation. What a fatal wandering! But *Abelard*, I have torn off the bandage which blinded me, and if I dare rely upon the emotions which I have felt, I have made myself worthy of your esteem. You are no more that amorous *Abelard*, who, to gain a private conversation with me by night, used incessantly to contrive new ways to deceive the vigilance of our observers. The misfortune, which happened to you after so many happy moments, gave you a horror for vice, and you instantly consecrated the rest of your days to virtue and seemed to submit to this necessity willingly. I indeed, more tender than you, and more sensible of soft pleasures, bore this misfortune with extreme impatience. You have heard my exclamations against your enemies; you have seen my whole resentment in those Letters I wrote to you; it was this, without doubt, which deprived me of the esteem of my *Abelard*. You were alarmed at my transport, and if you will confess the truth, you, perhaps, despaired of my salvation. You could not foresee that *Heloise* would conquer so reigning a passion; but you have been deceived, *Abelard*; my weakness, when supported by grace, hath not hindered me from obtaining a complete victory. Restore me, then, to your good opinion; your own piety ought to solicit you to this.

But what secret trouble rises in my soul, what unthought-of motion opposes the resolution I formed of sighing no more for *Abelard*? Just Heaven! have I not yet triumphed over my love? Unhappy *Heloise*! as long as thou drawest a breath it is decreed thou must love *Abelard*: weep unfortunate wretch that thou art, thou never had a more just occasion. Now I ought to die with grief. Grace had overtaken me, and I had promised to be faithful to it, but I now perjure myself, and sacrifice even grace to *Abelard*. This sacrilegious Sacrifice fills up the measure of my iniquities. After this can I hope God should open to me the treasures of his mercy? Have I not tired out his forgiveness? I began to offend him from the moment I first saw *Abelard*; an unhappy sympathy engaged us both in a criminal commerce; and God raised us up an enemy to separate us. I lament and hate the misfortune which hath lighted upon us and adore the cause. Ah! I ought rather to explain this accident as the secret ordinance of Heaven, which disapproved of our engagement, and apply myself to extirpate my passion. How much better were it entirely to forget the object of it, than to preserve the memory of it, so fatal to the quiet of my life and salvation? Great God! shall *Abelard* always possess my thoughts? can I never free myself from those chains which bind me to him? But, perhaps, I am unreasonably afraid; virtue directs all my motions, and they are all subject to grace, Fear no more, dear *Abelard*; I have no longer any of those sentiments which, being described in my Letters, have occasioned you so much trouble. I will no more endeavour, by the relation of those pleasures our new-born passion gave us, to awaken that criminal fondness you may have for me; I free you from all your oaths; forget the names of Lover and husband but keep always that of Father. I expect no more from you those tender protestations, and those letters so proper to keep up the commerce of love. I demand nothing of you but spiritual advice and wholesome directions. The path of holiness, however thorny it may be, will yet appear agreeable when I walk in your steps. You will always find me ready to follow you. I shall read with more pleasure the letters in which you shall describe to me the advantages of virtue than ever I did those by which you so artfully instilled the fatal poison of our passion. You cannot now be silent without a crime. When I was possessed with so violent a love, and pressed you so earnestly to write to me, how many letters did I send you before I could obtain one from you? You denied me in my misery the only comfort which was left me, because you thought it pernicious. You endeavoured by severities to force me to forget you; nor can I blame you; but now you have nothing to fear. A lucky disease which providence seemed to have chastised me with for my sanctification, hath done what all human efforts, and your cruelty in vain attempted. I see now the vanity of that happiness which we had set our hearts upon, as if we were never to have lost it. What fears, what uneasiness, have we been obliged to suffer!

No, Lord, there is no pleasure upon earth but that which virtue gives! The heart, amidst all worldly delights, feels a sting; it is uneasy and restless till fixed on thee. What have I not suffered, *Abelard*, while I kept alive in my retirement those fires which ruined me in the world? I saw with horror the walls which surrounded me; the hours seemed as long as years. I repented a thousand times the having buried myself here; but since grace has opened my eyes all the scene is changed. Solitude looks charming, and the tranquillity which I behold here enters my very heart. In the satisfaction of doing my duty I feel a pleasure above all that riches, pomp, or sensuality, could afford. My quiet has indeed cost me dear; I have bought it even at the price of my love; I have offered a violent sacrifice, and which seemed above my power. I have torn you from my heart; and, be not jealous, God reigns there in your stead, who ought always to have possessed it entire. Be content with having a place in my mind, which you shall never lose; I shall always take a secret pleasure in thinking of you and esteem it a glory to obey those rules you shall give me.

This very moment I receive a letter from you: I will read it, and answer it immediately. You shall see, by my exactness in writing to you, that you are always dear to me.—You very obligingly reproach me for delaying so long to write you any news; my illness must excuse that. I omit no opportunities of giving you marks of my remembrance. I thank you for the uneasiness you say my silence caused you, and the kind fears you express concerning my health. Yours, you tell me is but weakly, and you thought lately you should have died. With what indifference, cruel man! do you acquaint me with a thing so certain to afflict me? I told you in my former letter how unhappy I should be if you died; and if you loved me, you would moderate the rigour of your austere life. I represented to you the occasion I had for your advice, and consequently, the reason there was you should take care of yourself. But I will not tire you with the repetition of the same thing. *You desire us not to forget you in your prayers.* Ah! dear *Abelard*, you may depend upon the zeal of this society; it is devoted to you, and you cannot justly charge it with forgetfulness. You are our father, we your children; you are our guide, and we resign ourselves with assurance in your piety. We impose no pennance on ourselves but what you recommend, lest we should rather follow an indiscreet zeal than solid virtue. In a word, nothing is thought rightly done if without *Abelard's* approbation. You inform me of one thing that perplexes me, that you have heard that some of our sisters gave bad examples, and that there is a general looseness amongst them. Ought this to seem strange to you, who know how monasteries are filled now-a-days? Do fathers consult the inclinations of their children when they settle them? Are not interest and policy their only rules? This is the reason that monasteries are often filled with those who are a scandal to them. But I conjure you to tell me what are the irregularities you have heard of, and to teach me a proper remedy for them. I have not yet observed that looseness you mention; when I have, I will take due care. I walk my rounds every night, and make those I catch abroad return to their chambers; for I remember all the adventures which happened in the monasteries near Paris. You end your letter with a general deploring of your unhappiness, and wish for death as the end of a troublesome life. Is it possible a genius so great as yours should never get above his past misfortunes? What would the world say should they read your letters as I do? would they consider the noble motive of your retirement, or not rather think you had shut yourself up only to lament the condition to which my uncle's revenge had reduced you? What would your young pupils say who came so far to hear you, and prefer your severe lectures to the softness of a worldly life, if they should see you secretly a slave to your passions, and sensible of all those weakness from which your rules can secure them? This *Abelard* they so much admire, this great personage which guides them, would lose his fame,

~ 89 ~

and become the scorn of his pupils. If these reasons are not sufficient to give you constancy in your misfortunes, cast your eyes upon me, and admire my resolution of shutting myself up by your example. I was young when we were separated, and (if I dare believe what you were always telling me) worthy of any gentleman's affections. If I had loved nothing in *Abelard* but sensual pleasure, a thousand agreeable young men might have comforted me upon my loss of him. You know what I have done, excuse me therefore from repeating it. Think of those assurances I gave you of loving you with the utmost tenderness. I dried your tears with kisses; and because you were less powerful I became less reserved. Ah! if you had loved with delicacy the oaths I made, the transports I accompanied them with, the innocent caresses I profusely gave you, all this, sure, might have comforted you. Had you observed me to grow by degrees indifferent to you, you might have had reason to despair; but you never received greater marks of my passion than after that cruel revenge upon you.

Let me see no more in your letters, dear *Abelard*, such murmurs against Fortune; you are not the only one she has persecuted, and you ought to forget her outrages. What a shame is it for a philosopher not to be comforted for an accident which might happen to any man! Govern yourself by my example. I was born with violent passions; I daily strive with the most tender emotions, and glory in triumphing and subjecting them to reason. Must a weak mind fortify one that is so much superior? But whither am I transported? Is this discourse directed to my dear *Abelard*? one that practices all those virtues he teaches? If you complain of Fortune, it is not so much that you feel her strokes, as that you cannot show your enemies how much to blame they were in attempting to hurt you. Leave them, *Abelard*, to exhaust their malice, and continue to charm your auditors. Discover those treasures of learning Heaven seems to have reserved for you: your enemies, struck with the splendor of your reasoning, will do you justice. How happy should I be could I see all the world as entirely persuaded of your probity as I am! Your learning is allowed by all the world; your greatest enemies confess you are ignorant of nothing that the mind of man is capable of knowing.

My dear husband! (this is the last time I shall use that expression) shall I never see you again? shall I never have the pleasure of embracing you before death? What doth thou say, wretched *Heloise*? dost thou know what thou desirest? Canst thou behold those lovely eyes without recollecting those amorous glances which have been so fatal to thee? canst thou view that majestic air of *Abelard* without entertaining a jealousy of every one that sees so charming a man? that mouth, which cannot be looked upon without desire? In short all the person of *Abelard* cannot be viewed by any woman without danger. Desire therefore no more to see *Abelard*. If the memory of him has caused thee so much trouble, *Heloise*, what will not his presence do? what desires will it not excite in thy soul? how will it be possible for thee to keep thy reason at the sight of so amiable a man? I will own to you what makes the greatest pleasure I have in my retirement: After having passed the day in thinking of you, full of the dear idea, I give myself up at night to sleep. Then it is that *Heloise*, who dares not without trembling think of you by day, resigns herself entirely to the pleasure of hearing you and speaking to you. I see you, *Abelard*, and glut my eyes with the sight. Sometimes you entertain me with the story of your secret troubles and grievances, and create in me a sensible sorrow; sometimes forgetting the perpetual obstacles to our desires, you press me to make you happy, and I easily yield to your transports. Sleep gives you what your enemies rage has deprived you of; and our souls, animated with the same passion, are sensible of the same pleasure. But, oh! you delightful illusion, soft errors, how soon do you vanish away! At my awaking I open my eyes and see no *Abelard*; I stretch out my arm to take hold of him, but he is not there; I call him, he hears me not. What a fool am I to tell you my dreams, who are sensible of these pleasures? But do you, *Abelard*, never see *Heloise* in your sleep? how does she appear to you? do you entertain her with the same language as formerly when Fulbert committed her to your care? when you awake are you pleased or sorry? Pardon me; *Abelard*, pardon a mistaken lover. I must no more expect that vivacity from you which once animated all your actions. 'Tis no more time to require from you a perfect correspondence of desires. We have bound ourselves to severe austerities, and must follow them, let them cost us ever so dear. Let us think of our duties in these rigours, and make a good use of that necessity which keeps us separate. You *Abelard*, will happily finish your course; your desires and ambition will be no obstacles to your salvation. *Heloise* only must lament, she only must weep, without being certain whether all her tears will be available or not to her salvation.

I had like to have ended my letter without acquainting you with what happened here a few days ago. A young nun, who was one of those who are forced to take up with a convent without any examination. whether it will suit with their tempers or not, is by a stratagem I knew nothing of, escaped, and, as they say, fled with a young gentleman she was in love with into England. I have ordered all the house to conceal the matter. Ah, *Abelard*! if you were near us these disorders would not happen. All the sisters, charmed with seeing and hearing you, would think of nothing but practicing your rules and directions. The young nun had never formed so criminal a design as that of breaking her vows, had you been at our head to exhort us to live holily. If your eyes were witnesses of our actions, they would be innocent. When we slipt, you would lift us up, and establish us by your counsels; we should march with sure steps in the rough paths of virtue. I begin to perceive; *Abelard*, that I take too much pleasure in writing to you. I ought to burn my letter. It shows you I am still engaged in a deep passion for you, though at the beginning of it I designed to persuade you of the contrary. I am sensible of the motions both of grace and passion, and by turns yield to each. Have pity, *Abelard*, of the condition to which you have brought me, and make, in some measure, the latter days of my life as quiet as the first have been uneasy and disturbed.

Letter VI. Abelard to Heloise.

Abelard, having at last conquered the remains of his unhappy passion, had determined to put an end to so dangerous a correspondence as that between *Heloise* and himself. The following Letter therefore, though written with no less concern than his former, is free from mixtures of a worldly passion, and is full of the warmest sentiments of piety, and the most moving exhortations.

Write no more to me, *Heloise*; write no more to me; it is a time to end a commerce which makes our mortifications of no advantage to us. We retired from the world to sanctify ourselves; and by a conduit directly contrary to Christian morality, we become odious to Jesus Christ. Let us no more deceive ourselves; by flattering ourselves with the remembrance of our past pleasures, we shall make our lives troublesome, and we shall be incapable of relishing the sweets of solitude. Let us make a good use of our austerities, and no longer preserve the ideas of our crimes amongst the severities of penitence. Let a mortification of body and mind, a strick fasting, continual solitude, profound and holy meditations, and a sincere love of God, succeed our former irregularities.

Let us try to carry religious perfection to a very difficult point. 'Tis beautiful to find, in Christianity minds so disengaged from the earth, from the creatures and themselves, that they seem to act independently of those bodies they are joined to, and to use them as their slaves. We can never raise ourselves to too great heights when God is the object. Be our endeavours ever so great, they will always come short of reaching that exalted dignity, which even our apprehensions cannot reach. Let us act for God's glory, independent of the creatures or ourselves, without any regard to our own desires, or the sentiments of others. Were we in this temper of mind, *Heloise*, I would willingly make my abode at the Paraclete. My earnest care for a house I have founded would draw a thousand blessings on it. I would instruct it by my words, and animate it by my example. I would watch over the lives of my sisters, and would command nothing but what I myself would perform. I would direct you to pray,

meditate, labour and keep vows of silence; and I would myself pray,
meditate, labour and be silent.

However, when I spoke, it should be to lift you up when you
should fall, to strengthen you in your weaknesses, to enlighten you in
that darkness and obscurity which might at any time surprise you. I
would comfort you under those severities used by persons of great
virtue. I would moderate the vivacity of your zeal and piety, and give
your virtue an even temperament. I would point out those duties
which you ought to know, and satisfy you in those doubts which the
weakness of your reason might occasion. I would be your master and
father; and, by a marvellous talent, I would become lively, flow, soft
or severe, according to the different characters of those I should guide
in the painful path of Christian perfection.

But whither does my vain imagination carry me?

Ah? *Heloise*! how far are we from such a happy temper? Your
heart still burns with that fatal fire which you cannot extinguish, and
mine is full of trouble and uneasiness. Think not, *Heloise*, that I enjoy
here a perfect peace: I will, for the last time open my heart to you. I
am not yet disengaged from you; I fight against my excessive
tenderness for you; yet in spite of all endeavours, the remaining
fraility makes me but too sensible of your sorrows, and gives me a
share in them. Your Letters have indeed moved me; I could not read
with indifference characters wrote by that dear hand. I sigh, I weep,
and all my reason is, scarce sufficient to conceal my weakness from
my pupils. This, unhappy *Heloise*! is the miserable condition of
Abelard. The world, which generally errs in its notion, thinks I am
easy, and as if I had loved only in you the gratification of sense,
imagines I have now forgot you; but what a mistake is this! People,
indeed, did not mistake in thinking, when we separated, that shame
and grief for having been so cruelly used made me abandon the
world. It was not, as you know, a sincere repentance for having
offended God which inspired me with a design of retiring; however, I
considered the accident which happened to us as a secret design of
Providence to punish our crimes; and only looked upon Fulbert as the
instrument of Divine vengeance. Grace drew me into an asylum,
where I might yet have remained, if the rage of my enemies would
have permitted. I have endured all their persecutions, not doubting but
God himself raised them up in order to purify me.

When he saw me perfectly obedient to his holy will, he permitted that I should justify my doctrine. I made its purity public, and showed in the end that my faith was not only orthodox, but also perfectly clear from even the suspicion of novelty.

I should be happy if I had none to fear but my enemies, and no other hinderance to my salvation but their calumny: but, *Heloise*, you make me tremble. Your Letters declare to me that you are enslaved to a fatal passion; and yet if you cannot conquer it you cannot be saved; and what part would you have me take in this case? Would you have me stifle the inspirations of the Holy Ghost? shall I, to soothe you dry up those tears which the evil spirit makes you shed? Shall this be the fruit of my meditations? No; let us be more firm in our resolutions. We have not retired but in order to lament our sins, and to gain heaven; let us then resign ourselves to God with all our heart.

I know every thing in the beginning is difficult, but it is glorious to undertake the beginning of a great action, and that glory increases proportionably as the difficulties are more considerable. We ought upon this account to surmount bravely all obstacles which might hinder us in the practice of Christian virtue. In a monastery men are proved as gold in the furnace. No one can continue long there unless he bear worthily the yoke of our Lord.

Attempt to break those shameful chains which bind you to the flesh; and, if by the assistance of grace you are so happy as to accomplish this, I intreat you to think of me in your prayers. Endeavour with all your strength to be the pattern of a perfect Christian. It is difficult, I confess, but not impossible; and I expect this beautiful triumph from your teachable disposition. If your first endeavours prove weak, give not yourself up to despair; that would be cowardice: besides, I would have you informed, that you must necessarily take great pains; because you drive to conquer a terrible enemy, to extinguish raging fire, and to reduce to subjection your dearest affections. You must fight against your own desires; be not therefore pressed down with the weight of your corrupt nature: you have to do with a cunning adversary, who will use all means to seduce you; be always upon your guard; While we live we are exposed to temptations: this made a great saint say, that *the whole life of man was a temptation.* The devil, who never sleeps, walks continually around us, in order to surprise us on some unguarded side, and enters into our soul to destroy it.

However perfect any one may be, yet he may fall into temptations, and, perhaps, into such as may be useful. Nor is it wonderful that men should never be exempt from them, because he hath always within himself their force, concupiscence. Scarce are we delivered from one temptation, but another attacks us. Such is the lot of the posterity of Adam, that they should always have something to suffer, because they have forfeited their primitive happiness. We vainly flatter ourselves that we shall conquer temptations by flying; if we join not patience and humility, we shall torment ourselves to no purpose. We shall more certainly compass our end by imploring God's assistance than by using any means drawn from ourselves.

Be constant, *Heloise*; trust in God, and you will fall into few temptations: whenever they shall come, stifle them in their birth; let them not take root in your heart. Apply remedies to a disease, said an Ancient, in its beginning; for when it hath gained strength medicines will be unavailable. Temptations have their degrees; they are at first mere thoughts, and do not appear dangerous; the imagination receives them without any fears; a pleasure is formed out of them; we pause upon it, and at last we yield to it.

Do you now, *Heloise*, applaud my design of making you walk in the steps of the saints? do my words give you any relish for penitence? have you not remorse for your wanderings? and do you not wish you could like Magdalen, wash our Saviour's feet with your tears? If you have not these ardent emotions, pray that he would inspire them. I shall never cease to recommend you in my prayers, and always beseech him to assist you in your design of dying holily. You have quitted the world, and what object was worthy to detain you there? Lift up your eyes always to him so whom you have consecrated the rest of your days. Life upon this earth is misery. The very necessities to which our body is subject here are matter of affliction to a saint. *Lord,* said the Royal Prophet, *deliver me from my necessities*! They are wretched who do not know themselves for such, and yet they are more wretched who know their misery, and do not hate the corruption of the age. What fools are men to engage themselves to earthly things! they will be undeceived one day, and will know but too late how much they have been too blame in loving such false good. Persons truly pious do not thus mistake, they are disengaged from all sensual pleasures, and raise their desires to heaven. Begin *Heloise*; put your design in execution without delay; you have yet time enough to work out your salvation. Love Christ, and despise yourself for his sake. He would possess your heart, and be the sole object of your sighs and tears; seek for no comfort but in him. If you do not free yourself from me, you will fall with me; but if you quit me, and give up yourself to him, you will be stedfast and immoveable. If you force the Lord to forsake you, you will fall into distress; but if you be ever faithful to him, you will always be in joy. Magdalen wept, as thinking the Lord had forsaken her; but Martha said, See, the Lord calls you. Be diligent in your duty, and obey faithfully the motions of his grace, and Jesus will remain always with you.

Attend, *Heloise*, to some instructions I have to give you. You are at the head of a society, and you know there is this difference between those who lead a private life and such as are charged with the conduct of others; that the first need only labour for their own sanctification, and, in acquitting themselves of their duties, are not obliged to practise all the virtues in such an apparent manner; whereas they who have the conduct of others intruded to them, ought by their example to engage them to do all the good they are capable of in their condition. I beseech you to attend to this truth, and so to follow it, as that your whole life may be a perfect model of that of a religious recluse.

God, who heartily desires our salvation, hath made all the means of it easy to us; In the *Old Testament* he hath written in the Tables of the Law what he requires of us, that we might not be bewildered in seeking after his will. In the *New Testament* he hath written that law of grace in our hearts, to the intent that it might be always present with us; and, knowing the weakness and incapacity of our nature, he hath given us grace to perform his will; and, as if this were not enough, he hath, at all times, in all dates of the church, raised up men who, by their exemplary life, might excite others to their duty. To effect this, he hath chosen persons of every age, sex, and condition. Strive now to unite in yourself all those virtues which have been scattered in these different states. Have the purity of virgins, the austerity of anchorites, the zeal of pastors and bishops, and the constancy of martyrs. Be exact in the course of your whole life to fulfil the duties of a holy and enlightened superior, and then death, which is commonly considered as terrible, will appear agreeable to you.

The death of his saints, says the Prophet, *is precious in the sight of the Lord.* Nor is it difficult to comprehend why their death should have this advantage over that of sinners. I have remarked three things which might have given the Prophet an occasion of speaking thus. First, Their resignation to the will of God. Secondly, The continuation of their good works. And, lastly, The triumph they gain over the devil.

A saint, who has accustomed himself to submit to the will of God, yields to death without reluctance. He waits with joy (says St. Gregory) for the Judge who is to reward him; he fears not to quit this miserable mortal life, in order to begin an immortal happy one. It is not so with the sinner, says the same Father; he fears, and with reason, he trembles, at the approach of the least sickness; death is terrible to him, because he cannot bear the presence of an offended Judge; and having so often abused the grace of God, he sees no way to avoid the punishment due to his sins.

The saints have besides this advantage over sinners that having made works of piety familiar to them during their life, they exercise them without trouble, and having gained new strength against the devil every time they overcome him, they will find themselves in a condition at the hour of death to obtain that victory over him, on which depends all eternity, and the blessed union of their souls with their Creator.

I hope, *Heloise*, that after having deplored the irregularities of your past life, you will die (as the Prophet prayed) the death of the righteous. Ah! how few are there who make their end after this manner! and why? It is because there are so few who love the Cross of Christ. Every one would be saved, but few will use those means which Religion prescribes. And yet we can be saved by nothing but the Cross, why then do we refuse to bear it? Hath not our Saviour borne it before us, and died for us, to the end that we might also bear it and desire to die also? All the saints have been afflicted; and our Saviour himself did not pass one hour of his life without some sorrow. Hope not, therefore to be exempted from sufferings. The

Cross, *Heloise*, is always at hand, but take care that you do not bear it with regret; for by so doing you will make it more heavy, and you will be oppressed by it unprofitably. On the contrary, if you bear it with affection and courage, all your sufferings will create in you a holy confidence, whereby you will find comfort in God. Hear our Saviour who says: "My child renounce yourself, take up your cross and follow me." Oh, *Heloise*! do you doubt? Is not your soul ravished at so saving a command? are you deaf to his voice? are you insensible to words so full of kindness? Beware, *Heloise*, of refusing a husband who demands you, and is more to be feared, if you slight his affection, than any profane lover. Provoked at your contempt and ingratitude, he will turn his love into anger, and make you feel his vengeance, How will you sustain his presence when you shall stand before his tribunal? He will reproach you for having despised his grace; he will represent to you his sufferings for you. What answer can you make? he will then be implacable. He will say to you, Go, proud creature, dwell in everlasting flames. I separated you from the world to purify you in solitude, and you did not second my design; I endeavoured to save you, and you took pains to destroy yourself; go wretch, and take the portion of the reprobates.

Oh, *Heloise*, prevent these terrible words, and avoid by a holy course, the punishment prepared for sinners. I dare not give you a description of those dreadful torments which ere the consequences of a life of guilt. I am filled with horror when they offer themselves to my imagination: and yet *Heloise* I can conceive nothing which can reach the tortures of the damned. The fire which we see upon earth is but the shadow of that which burns them; and without enumerating their endless pains, the loss of God which they feel increases all their torments. Can any one sin who is persuaded of this? My God! can we dare to offend thee? Tho' the riches of thy mercy could not engage us to love thee, the dread of being thrown into such an abyss of misery would restrain us from doing any thing which might displease thee?

I question not, *Heloise*, but you will hereafter apply yourself in good earnest to the business of your salvation: this ought to be your whole concern. Banish me, therefore, for ever from your heart; it is the best advice I can give you: for the remembrance of a person we have loved criminally cannot but be hurtful, whatever advances we have made in the ways of virtue. When you have extirpated your unhappy inclination towards me, the practice of every virtue will become easy; and when at last your life is conformable to that of Christ, death will be desireable to you. Your soul will joyfully leave this body, and direct its flight to heaven. Then you will appear with confidence before your Saviour. You will not read characters of your reprobation written in the book of life; but you will hear your Saviour say, Come, partake of my glory, and enjoy the eternal reward I have appointed for those virtues you have practised.

Farewell *Heloise*. This is the last advice of your dear *Abelard*; this is the last time, let me persuade you to follow the holy rules of the Gospel. Heaven grant that your heart, once so sensible of my love, may now yield to be directed by my zeal! May the idea of your loving *Abelard*, always present to your mind, be now changed into the image of *Abelard* truly penitent! and may you shed as many tears for your salvation as you have done during the course of our misfortunes!

Eloisa to Abelard by Mr Pope.

In these deep solitudes and awful cells.
Where heav'nly-pensive Contemplation dwells,
And ever-musing Melancholy reigns;
What means this tumult in a Vestal's veins?
Why rove my thoughts beyond this last retreat?
Why feels my heart its long-forgotten beat?
Yet, yet I love!——From *Abelard* it came,
And *Eloisa* yet must kiss the name.
　　　　Dear fatal name! rest ever onreveal'd,
Nor pass those lips in holy silence seas'd:
Hide it, my heart, within that close disguise,
Where mix'd with God's, his lov'd idea lyes;
Oh write it not, my hand—the name appears
Already written—wash it out, my tears!
In vain lost *Eloisa* weeps and prays,
Her heart still dictates, and her hand obeys.
　　　　Relentless walls! whose darksome round contains
Repentant sighs, and voluntary pains:
Ye rugged rocks! which holy knees have worn;
Ye grotes and caverns shagg'd with horrid thorn!
Shrines! where their vigils pale-ey'd virgins keep,
And pitying saints, whose statues learn to weep!
Tho' cold like you unmov'd and silent grown,
I have not yet forgot myself to stone.
Heav'n claims me all in vain, while he has part,
Still rebel Nature holds out half my heart;
Nor pray'rs nor fasts its stubborn pulse restrain,
Nor tears, for ages taught to flow in vain.
　　　　Soon as thy Letters, trembling, I unclose,
That well-known name awakens all my woes.
Oh name for ever sad! for ever dear!
Still breath'd in sighs, still utter'd with a tear.
I tremble too where'er my own I find,
Some dire misfortune follows close behind.
Line after line my gushing eyes o'erflow,

Pierre Abelard

Led through a sad variety of woe:
Now warm in love, now with'ring in thy bloom,
Lost in a convent's solitary gloom!
There stern religion quench'd th' unwilling flame.
There died the best of passions, love and same.

      Yet write, oh write me all, that I may join
Griefs to thy griefs, and echo sighs to thine.
Nor foes nor fortune take this pow'r away;
And is my *Abelard* less kind than they?
Tears still are mine, and those I need not spare,
Love but demands what else were shed in pray'r;
No happier talk these faded eyes pursue;
To read and weep is all they now can do.

      Then share thy pain, allow that sad relief;
Ah, more than share it! give me all thy grief.
Heav'n first taught letters for some wretch's aid,
Some banish'd lover, or some captive maid;
They live they speak, they breathe what love inspires,
Warm from the soul, and faithful to its fires,
The virgin's wish without her fears impart,
Excuse the blush, and pour out all the heart,
Speed the soft intercourse from soul to soul,
And waft a sigh from Indus to the Pole.

      Thou know'st how guiltless first I met thy flame,
When Love approach'd me under Friendship's name;
My fancy form'd thee of angelic kind,
Some emanations of th' all-beauteous Mind.
Those smiling eyes, attemp'ring every ray,
Shone sweetly lambent with celestial day.
Guiltless I gaz'd; Heav'n listen'd while you sung;
And truths divine came mended from that tongue,
From lip like those what precepts fail'd to move?
Too soon they taught me 'twas no sin to love:
Back through the paths of pleasing sense I ran,
Nor wish'd an angel whom I lov'd a man.
Dim and remote the joys of saints I see,
Nor envy them that heav'n I lose for thee.

      How oft', when prest to marriage, have I said,
Curse on all laws but those which Love has made!

Love, free as air, at sight of human ties,
Spreads his light wings, and in a moment flies.
Let wealth, let honour, wait the wedded dame,
August her deed, and sacred be her fame;
Before true passion all those views remove,
Fame, wealth, and honour! what are you to love?
The jealous God, when we profane his fires,
Those restless passions in revenge inspires,
And bids them make mistaken mortals groan,
Who seek in love for ought but love alone.
Should at my feet the world's great master fall,
Himself, his throne, his world, I'd scorn 'em all;
Not *Ceasar's* empress would I deign to prove;
No, make me mistress to the man I love;
If there be yet another name more free,
More fond, than Mistress, make me that to thee!
Oh happy state! when souls each other draw.
When love is liberty, and nature law,
All then is full possessing and possess'd,
No craving void left akeing in the breast?
Ev'n thought meets thought, ere from the lips it part,
And each warm wish springs mutual from the heart.
This sure is bliss, (if bliss on earth there be,)
And once the lot of *Abelard* and me.

Alas, how chang'd! what sudden horrors rise!
A naked lover bound and bleeding lyes!
Where, where was *Eloisa*? her voice, her hand,
Her poinard, had oppos'd the dire command.
Barbarian, stay! that bloody stroke restrain;
The crime was common, common be the pain.
I can no more; by shame, by rage, suppress'd,
Let tears and burning blushes speak the rest.

Canst thou forget that sad, that solemn day,
When victims at yon altar's foot we lay?
Canst thou forget what tears that moment fell,
When, warm in youth, I bade the world farewell?
As, with cold lips I kiss'd the sacred veil,
The shrines all trembled, and the lamps grew pale:

Pierre Abelard

Heav'n scarces believ'd the conquest it survey'd,
And saints with wonder heard the vows I made.
Yet then, to those dread altars as I drew,
Not on the Cross my eyes were fix'd, but you:
Not grace, or zeal, love only was my call,
And if I lose thy love, I lose my all.
Come! with thy looks, thy words, relieve my woe;
Those still at least are left thee to bestow.
Still on that breast enamour'd let me lye,
Still drink delicious poison from thy eye,
Pant on thy lip, and to thy heart be press'd;
Give all thou canst——and let me dream the rest,
Ah, no! instruct me other joys to prize,
With other beauties charm my partial eyes.
Full in my view set all the bright abode,
And make my soul quit *Abelard* for God.

Ah! think at least thy flock deserves thy care,
Plants of thy hand, and children of thy pray'r.
From the false world in early youth they fled,
By thee to mountains, wilds, and deserts led.
You rais'd these hallow'd walls; the desart smil'd,
And Paradise was open'd in the wild.
No weeping orphan saw his father's stores
Our shines irradiate, or emblaze the floors:
No silver saints, by dying misers given,
Here brib'd the rage of ill-requited Heav'n:
But such plain roofs as piety could raise,
And only vocal with the maker's praise.
In these lone walls (their days eternal bound)
These moss-grown domes with spiry turrets crown'd,
Where awful arches make a noon-day night,
And the dim windows shed a solemn light;
Thy eyes diffus'd a reconciling ray,
And gleams of glory brighten'd all the day,
But now no face divine contentment wears,
'Tis all blank sadness, or continual tears.
See how the force of others' pray'rs I try,
(Oh pious fraud of am'rous charity!)
But why should I on others' prayers depend?

Come thou, my Father, Brother, Husband, Friend!
Ah, let thy Handmaid, Sister, Daughter, move,
And all those tender Names in one, thy Love!
The darksome pines, that o'er yon rocks reclin'd
Wave high, and murmur to the hollow wind,
The wand'ring streams that shine between the hills,
The grotes that echo to the tinkling rills,
The dying gales that pant upon the trees,
The lakes that quiver to the curling breeze;
No more these scenes my meditation aid,
Or lull to rest the visionary maid.
But o'er the twilight groves, and dusky caves,
Long founding aisles, and intermingled graves,
Black Melancholy sits, and round her throws
A death like silence, and a dread repose:
Her gloomy presence saddens all the scene.
Shades ev'ry flow'r, and darkens ev'ry green,
Deepens the murmur of the falling floods,
And breathes a browner horror on the woods,

       Yet here for ever, ever must I stay;
Sad proof how well a lover can obey!
Death, only death, can break the lasting chain;
And here, ev'n then, shall my cold dust remain;
Here all its frailties, all its flames resign,
And wait, till 'tis no sin to mix with thine.

       Ah, wretch! believ'd the spouse of God in vain,
Confess'd within the slave of love and man.
Assist me, Heav'n! But whence, arose that pray'r?
Sprung it from piety, or from despair?
Ev'n here, where frozen Chastity retires,
Love finds an altar for forbidden fires.
I ought to grieve, but cannot what I ought;
I mourn the lover, not lament the fault;
I view my crime, but kindle at the view,
Repent old pleasures, and solicit new;
Now turn'd to Heav'n, I weep my past offence,
Now think of thee, and curse my innocence.
Of all Affliction taught a lover yet,
'Tis sure the hardest science to forget!

How shall I lose the sin, yet, keep the sense.
And love th' offender, yet detest th' offence?
How the dear object from the crime remove,
Or how distinguish penitence from love?
Unequal talk! a passion to resign,
For hearts so touched, so pierc'd, so lost as mine.
Ere such a soul regains its peaceful slate.
How often must it love, how often hate!
How often hope, despair, resent, regret.
Conceal, disdain—do all things but forget!
But let Heav'n seize it, all at once 'tis fir'd,
Not touched but rapt; not waken'd but inspir'd!
Oh come! oh teach me nature to subdue.
Renounce my love, my life, myself—and you.
Fill my fond heart with God alone, for he
Alone can rival, can succeed to thee.

How happy is the blameless Vestal's lot?
The world forgetting, by the world forgot:
Eternal sunshine of the spotless mind!
Each pray'r accepted, and each wish resign'd;
Labour and rest, that equal periods keep,
'Obedient slumbers that can wake and weep;
Desires compos'd, affections ever even;
Tears that delight, and sighs that waft to heav'n.
Grace shines around her with serenest beams,
And whisp'ring angels prompt her golden dreams,
For her the house prepares the bridal ring,
For her white virgins *hymeneals* sing,
For her th' unfading rose of Eden blooms,
And wings of seraphs shed divine perfumes;
To sounds of heavenly harps she dies away,
And melts in visions of eternal day.
Far other dreams my erring soul employ,
Far other raptures of unholy joy:
When at the close of each sad sorrowing day
Fancy restores what Vengeance snatch'd away,
Then Conscience sleeps, and leaving Nature free,
All my loose soul unbounded springs to thee.
O curs'd dear horrors of all-conscious Night!

How glowing guilt exalts the keen delight!
Provoking daemons all restraint remove,
And stir within me ev'ry source of love,
I hear thee, view thee, gaze o'er all thy charms,
And round thy phantoms glue my clasping arms.
I wake——no more I hear, no more I view,
The phantom flies me as unkind as you.
I call aloud; it hears not what I say;
I stretch my empty arms; it glides away.
To dream once more I close my willing eyes;
Ye soft illusions, dear deceits, arise!
Alas no more!——Methinks we wand'ring go,
Thro' dreary waftes, and weep each other's woe
Where round some moulding tow'r pale ivy creeps,
And low-brow'd rocks hang nodding o'er the deeps.
Sudden you mount, you beckon from the skies:
Clouds interpose, waves roar, and winds arise.
I shriek, start up, the same sad prospect find
And wake to all the griefs I left behind.

      For thee the fates, severely kind, ordain
A cool suspence from pleasure and from pain;
Thy life a long dead calm of fix'd repose;
No pulse that riots, and no blood that glows;
Still as the sea, ere winds were taught to blow,
Or moving Spirit bade the waters flow;
Soft as the slumbers of a saint forgiv'n,
And mild as opening gleams of promis'd heav'n.
      Come, *Abelard*! for what hast thou to dread?
The torch of Venus burns not for the dead.
Nature stands check'd; Religion disapproves;
Ev'n thou art cold——yet *Eloisa* loves.
Ah hopeless, lasting flames! like those that burn.
To light the dead, and warm th' unfruitful urn.
What scenes appear! where e'er I turn my view.
The dear ideas where I fly pursue,
Rise in the grove, before the altar rise,
Stain all my soul, and wanton in my eyes.
I waste the matin lamp in sighs for thee,
Thy image steals between my God and me;

Pierre Abelard

Thy voice I seem in ev'ry hymn to hear,
With ev'ry bead I drop too soft a tear.
When from the censer clouds of fragrance roll,
And swelling organs lift the rising soul,
One thought of thee puts all the pomp to flight,
Priests, tapers, temples; swim before my sight:
In seas of flame my plunging soul is drown'd,
While altars blaze, and angels tremble round.
While prostrate here in humble grief I lye
Kind, virtuous drops, just gathering in my eye,
While praying, trembling, in the dust I roll,
And dawning grace is opening on my soul:
Come, if thou dar'st, all charming as thou art!
Oppose thyself to Heav'n; dispute my heart;
Come, with one glance of those deluding eyes
Blot out each bright idea of the skies;
Take back that grace, those sorrows, and those tears;
Take back my fruitless penitence and prayers;
Snatch me, just mounting, from the blest abode;
Assist the fiend, and tear me from my God!

No, fly me! fly me! far as pole from pole;
Rise Alps between us, and whose oceans roll!
Ah, come not, write not, think not once of me,
Nor share one pang of all I felt for thee,
Thy oaths I quit, thy memory resign;
Forget, renounce me, hate whate'er was mine.
Fair eyes, and tempting looks, which yet I view!
Long-liv'd ador'd ideas, all adieu!
O grace serene! oh virtue heav'nly fair!
Divine oblivion of low-thoughted care!
Fresh blooming Hope, gay daughter of the sky!
And faith, our early immortality!
Enter, each mild, each amicable guest;
Receive and wrap me in eternal rest!
  See in her cell sad *Eloisa* spread,
Propt on some tomb, a neighbour of the dead!
In each low wind methinks a spirit calls,
And more than echoes talk along the walls,
Here, as I watch'd the dying lamps around,

Letters of Abelard and Heloise

From yonder shrine I heard a hollow sound:
'Come, sister, come I (it said, or seem'd to say,)
'Thy place is here, sad sister come away!
'Once like thyself I trembled, wept, and pray'd,
'Love's victim then, though now a sainted maid:
'But all is calm in this eternal sleep;
'Here Grief forgets to groan, and Love to weep;
'Ev'n Superstition loses ev'ry fear:
'For God, not man, absolves our frailties here.'

        I come, I come! prepare your roseat bow'rs,
Celestial palm, and ever-blooming flow'rs.
Thither, were sinners may have rest, I go,
Where flames refin'd in breasts seraphic glow:
Thou, *Abelard*! the last sad office pay,
And smooth my passage to the realms of day;
See my lips tremble, and my eye-balk roll,
Suck my last breath, and catch the flying soul!
Ah no——in sacred vestments may'st thou stand,
The hallow'd taper trembling in thy hand,
Present the Cross before my lifted eye,
Teach me at once, and learn of me to die.
Ah then, the once lov'd *Eloisa* see!
It will be then no crime to gaze on me.
See from my cheek the transient roses fly!
See the last sparkle languish in my eye!
'Till ev'ry motion, pulse, and breath be o'er;
And ev'n my *Abelard.* be lov'd no more.
O death, all eloquent! you only prove
What dust we dote on, when 'tis man we love.
   Then too, when Fate shall thy fair frame destroy?
(That cause of all my guilt, and all my joy)
In trance ecstatic may the pangs be drown'd,
Bright clouds descend, and angels watch thee round,
From opening skies may streaming glories shine,
And saints embrace thee with a love like mine.

        May one kind grave unite each hapless name,
And graft my love immortal on thy fame!
Then, ages hence, when all my woes are o'er,

Pierre Abelard

When this rebellious heart shall beat no more.
If ever Chance two wand'ring lovers brings
To *Paraclete's* white walls and silver springs,
O'er the pale marble shall they join their heads.
And drink the falling tears each other sheds;
Then sadly say, with mutual pity mov'd,
"Oh may we never love as these have lov'd!"
From the full choir, when loud Hosannas rise,
And swell the pomp of dreadful sacrifice,
Amid that scene, if some relenting eye
Glance on the stone where our cold relics lye,
Devotion's self shall steal a thought from heav'n,
One human tear shall drop, and be forgiven.
And sure, if Fate some future bard shall join
In sad similitude of griefs like mine,
Condemn'd whole years in absence to deplore,
And image charms he must behold no more;
Such if there be, who loves so long, so well;
Let him our sad, our tender, story tell;
The well-sung woes will smooth my pensive ghost:
He best can paint e'm, who shall feel 'em most.

Abelard to Eloisa by Mrs Madan.

In my dark cell, low prostrate on the ground,
Mourning my crimes, thy Letter entrance found;
Too soon my soul the well-known name confest,
My beating heart sprang fiercely in my breast,
Thro' my whole frame a guilty transport glow'd,
And streaming torrents from my eyes fast flow'd:
  O *Eloisa*! art thou still the same?
Dost thou still nourish this destructive flame?
Have not the gentle rules of Peace and Heav'n,
From thy soft soul this fatal passion driv'n?
Alas! I thought you disengaged and free;
And can you still, still sigh and weep for me?
What powerful Deity, what hallow'd Shrine,
Can save me from a love, a faith like thine?
Where shall I fly, when not this awful Cave,
Whose rugged feet the surging billows lave;
When not these gloomy cloister's solemn walls,
O'er whose rough sides the languid ivy crawls,
When my dread vews, in vain, their force oppose?
Oppos'd to live—alas!—how vain are vows!
In fruitless penitence I wear away
Each tedious night, and sad revolving day;
I fast, I pray, and, with deceitful art,
Veil thy dear image in my tortur'd heart;
My tortur'd heart conflicting passions move.
I hope despair, repent——yet still I love:
A thousand jarring thoughts my bosom tear;
For, thou, not God, O *Eloise!* art there.
To the false world's deluding pleasures dead,
Nor longer by its wand'ring fires misled,
In learn'd disputes harsh precepts I infuse,
And give the counsel I want pow'r to use.
The rigid maxims of the grave and wife
Have quench'd each milder sparkle of my eyes:
Each lovley feature of this once lov'd face,

By grief revers'd, assumes a sterner grace;
O *Eloisa*! should the fates once more,
Indulgent to my view, thy charms restore,
How from my arms would'st thou with horror start
To miss the form familiar to thy heart;
Nought could thy quick, thy piercing judgment see,
To speak me *Abelard*—but love to thee.
Lean Abstinence, pale Grief, and haggard Care.
The dire attendants of forlorn Despair,
Have *Abelard*, the young, the gay, remov'd,
And in the Hermit funk the man you lov'd,
Wrapt in the gloom these holy mansions shed,
The thorny paths of Penitence I tread;
Lost to the world, from all its int'rests free,
And torn from all my soul held dear in thee,
Ambition with its train of frailties gone,
All loves and forms forget——but thine alone,
Amid the blaze of day, the dusk of night,
My *Eloisa* rises to my sight;
Veil'd as in Paraclete's secluded tow'rs,
The wretched mourner counts the lagging hours;
I hear her sighs, see the swift falling tears,
Weep all her griefs, and pant with all her cares.
O vows! O convent! your stern force impart,
And frown the melting phantom from my heart;
Let other sighs a worthier sorrow show,
Let other tears from sin repentance flow;
Low to the earth my guilty eyes I roll,
And humble to the dust my heaving soul,
Forgiving Pow'r! thy gracious call I meet,
Who first impower'd this rebel heart to heart;
Who thro' this trembling, this offending frame,
For nobler ends inspir'd life's active flame.
O! change the temper of this laboring breast,
And form anew each beating pulse to rest!
Let springing grace, fair faith, and hope remove
The fatal traces of destructive love!
Destructive love from his warm mansions tear,
And leave no traits of *Eloisa* there!

Letters of Abelard and Heloise

Are these the wishes of my inmost soul?
Would I its soft, its tend'rest sense controul?
Would I, thus touch'd, this glowing heart refine,
To the cold substance of this marble shrine?
Transform'd like these pale swarms that round me move,
Of blest insensibles—who know no love?
Ah! rather let me keep this hapless flame;
Adieu! false honour, unavailing fame!
Not your harsh rules, but tender love, supplies
The streams that gush from my despairing eyes;
I feel the traitor melt about my heart,
And thro' my veins with treacherous influence dart;
Inspire me, Heav'n! assist me, Grace divine,
Aid me, ye Saints! unknown to pains like mine;
You, who on earth serene all griefs could prove,
All but the tort'ring pangs of hopeless love;
A holier rage in your pure bosoms dwelt,
Nor can you pity what you never felt:
A sympathising grief alone can lure,
The hand that heals, must feel what I endure.
Thou, *Eloise* alone canst give me ease,
And bid my struggling soul subside to peace;
Restore me to my long lost heav'n of rest,
And take thyself from my reluctant breast;
If crimes like mine could an allay receive,
That blest allay thy wond'rons charms might give.
Thy form, that first to love my heart inclin'd,
Still wanders in my lost, my guilty mind.
I saw thee as the new blown blossoms fair,
Sprightly as light, more soft than summer's air,
Bright as their beams thy eyes a mind disclose,
Whilst on thy lips gay blush'd the fragrant rose;
Wit, youth, and love, in each dear feature shone;
Prest by my fate, I gaz'd—and was undone.
There dy'd the gen'rous fire, whose vig'rous flame
Enlarged my soul, and urg'd me on to same;
Nor fame, nor wealth, my soften'd heart could move,
Dully insensible to all but love.
Snatch'd from myself, my learning tasteless grew;
Vain my philosophy, oppos'd to you;

A train of woes succeed, nor should we mourn,
The hours that cannot, ought not to return.

As once to love I sway'd your yielding mind,
Too fond, alas! too fatally inclin'd,
To virtue now let me your breast inspire,
And fan, with zeal divine, the heav'nly fire;
Teach you to injur'd Heav'n all chang'd to turn,
And bid the soul with sacred rapture burn.
O! that my own example might impart
This noble warmth to your soft trembling heart!
That mine, with pious undissembled care,
Could aid the latent virtue struggling there;

Alas! I rave—nor grace, nor zeal divine,
Burn in a heart oppress'd with crimes like mine,
Too sure I find, while I the tortures prove
Of feeble piety, conflicting love,
On black despair my forc'd devotion's built;
Absence for me has sharper pangs than guilt.
Yet, yet, my *Eloisa*, thy charms I view,
Yet my sighs breath, my tears pour forth for you;
Each weak resistance stronger knits my chain,
I sigh, weep, love, despair, repent——in vain,
Haste, *Eloisa*, haste, your lover free,
Amidst your warmest pray'r——O think on me!
Wing with your rising zeal my grov'ling mind,
And let me mine from your repentance find!
Ah! labour, strife, your love, your self control!
The change will sure affect my kindred soul;
In blest consent our purer sighs shall breath,
And Heav'n assisting, shall our crimes forgive,
But if unhappy, wretched, lost in vain,
Faintly th' unequal combat you sustain;
If not to Heav'n you feel your bosom rise,
Nor tears refin'd fall contrite from your eyes;
If still, your heart its wonted passions move,
If still, to speak all pains in one—you love;
Deaf to the weak essays of living breath,
Attend the stronger eloquence of Death.

When that kind pow'r this captive soul shall free,
Which only then can cease to doat on thee;
When gently sunk to my eternal sleep,
The Paraclete my peaceful urn shall keep!
Then, *Eloisa*, then your lover view,
See his quench'd eyes no longer gaze on you;
From their dead orbs that tender utt'rance flown,
Which first to thine my heart's soft fate made known,
This breast no more, at length to ease consign'd,
Pant like the waving aspin in the wind;
See all my wild, tumultuous passion o'er,
And thou, amazing change! belov'd no more;
Behold the destin'd end of human love—
But let the fight your zeal alone improve;
Let not your conscious soul, to sorrow mov'd,
Recall how much, how tenderly I lov'd:
With pious care your fruitless griefs restrain,
Nor let a tear your sacred veil profane;
Not ev'n a sigh on my cold urn bestow;
But let your breast with new-born raptures glow;
Let love divine, frail mortal love dethrone,
And to your mind immortal joys make known;
Let Heav'n relenting strike your ravish'd view,
And still the bright, the blest pursuit renew!
So with your crimes shall your misfortune cease,
And your rack'd soul be calmly hush'd to peace.

The Meaning of Life and Other Useless Crap is perhaps our generations greatest work as it answers the age old question "What is the meaning of life?" Written simply and straightforward it is easy to understand why Ben Lemon is the most important living philosopher. It hasn't been since A Modest Proposal that a pamphlet can our perceptions so dramatically.

47836150R00068

Made in the USA
Middletown, DE
10 June 2019